MW00781941

"Preachers like me need t[...]
think of anyone I'd rather [...]
process than Rick Reed. While he understands the need for careful
exegesis and a clear, compelling outline, he knows that a preacher's
biggest challenge is doing the heart work needed to preach a life-
transforming sermon. There's so much helpful counsel in The Heart of
the Preacher on everything from redeeming ambition to dealing with
Blue Mondays to practicing soul care to making the most of Saturday
nights. I plan to require this book for the preaching classes I teach.
First, though, I need to read it again to prepare my heart for the task
of proclaiming God's Word."

—**Steven D. Mathewson**, pastor,
Crosslife Evangelical Free Church (Libertyville, IL);
Director of the Doctor of Ministry program at
Western Seminary (Portland, OR); author of
The Art of Preaching Old Testament Narrative

"There are plenty of books to teach you how to prepare a sermon, but
there are few books that will teach you how to prepare your heart to
preach a sermon. Building out of a lifetime's experience, Rick Reed
has addressed this extra level of mastery in preaching. Your heart is
worth paying attention to, and so is this book."

—**Kenton C. Anderson**,
President and Professor of Homiletics,
Northwest Baptist Seminary;
author of Integrative Preaching

"In The Heart of the Preacher, Rick Reed comes alongside preachers
to encourage and challenge them to reach their potential and fulfill
their high calling. As you read this book you will benefit from Reed's
wisdom, but more than that, you will encounter his heart—a heart that
beats with grace and truth."

—**Jim L. Wilson**,
Professor of Leadership Formation and
Doctor of Ministry Director,
Gateway Seminary

"*The Heart of the Preacher* is as easy to read as it is hard to hear. With refreshing and unrelenting honesty, Rick Reed gifts those of us who preach with a disturbingly accurate MRI of our souls, and then helpfully guides us forward. Every pastor needs to buy this book. And give a copy to a colleague."

—**J. Kent Edwards**,
Professor of Preaching and Leadership,
Talbot School of Theology;
Founder/CEO, CrossTalk Global

"Speaking in a pastoral tone to today's preachers, Rick Reed helps identify, examine, and navigate the inner conflictedness of public ministry, which involves gaining a reputation while pointing to another—proclaiming boldly while making clear what is better and who is greater than the proclaimer. Reed fills a gaping hole in current homiletics literature on the spiritual dynamics of sermon preparation, and generously sprinkles practical hints on the mechanics of an effective sermon too. This book will be a required text in my course on spiritual preparation for preaching."

—**Ramesh Richard**, President,
Ramesh Richard Evangelism and Church Health (RREACH);
Professor, Global Theological Engagement and
Pastoral Ministries, Dallas Theological Seminary

"Henri Nouwen once said, 'If we don't have a hidden life with God, our public life for God cannot bear fruit.' This thoughtful book is a useful tool for encouraging and equipping preachers toward this end. I'm thankful for Rick Reed's desire to help develop healthy and sustainable ministers of the gospel."

—**Curtis Zackery**, author of *Soul Rest:
Reclaim Your Life; Return to Sabbath*

The HEART of the PREACHER

THE HEART
of the
PREACHER

Preparing Your Soul to Proclaim the Word

Rick Reed

LEXHAM PRESS

The Heart of the Preacher: Preparing Your Soul to Proclaim the Word

Copyright 2019 Rick Reed

Lexham Press, 1313 Commercial St., Bellingham, WA 98225
LexhamPress.com

All rights reserved. You may use brief quotations from this resource in presentations, articles, and books. For all other uses, please write Lexham Press for permission. Email us at permissions@lexhampress.com.

Unless otherwise noted, Scripture quotations are from *ESV® Bible* (*The Holy Bible, English Standard Version®*), copyright 2001 by Crossway Bibles, a publishing ministry of Good News Publishers. Used by permission. All rights reserved.

Paperback ISBN 9781683598411
Digital ISBN 9781683593492

Lexham Editorial Team: Elliot Ritzema, Jennifer Edwards, Danielle Thevenaz
Cover Design: George Siler
Typesetting: Scribe Inc.

24 25 26 27 28 29 30 / US / 12 11 10 9 8 7 6 5 4 3 2 1

To my preaching models and mentors:

Maynor Reed

Bill Lawrence

and Bill McRae

CONTENTS

FOREWORD

Much has been written about pastoral "burnout" in recent years, but this is not the first generation of pastors to look for the exit sign from spiritual leadership. When congregational challenges, personal attack, and inescapable fatigue dug into Moses' heart, he also walked from the path God had designed for his ministry (Num 20:1–13).

Commenting on the Israelite leader's response, the psalmist says that Moses used "rash" words (Ps 106:33). In plain terms, Moses got mad, causing him to lash out at those who had hurt him and to dishonor the God who had helped him.

How did it happen? Moses had been faithful for so many decades. He had been brave when others ran. He had relied on God when others turned to idols. He had followed the cloud and fire of God's direction when others wanted to go back to Egypt. Moses had led well for more than forty years by providing God's instruction for behavior, belief, and the nation's direction. Why, then, did he falter so late in the journey toward the promised land?

THE MOSES FACTOR

We won't get to the answer if we suggest the reason is the same as researchers gave for pastoral burnout a decade ago. At that time, roughly thirty percent of all North American seminary graduates were leaving pastorates within the first five years of ministry.

Researchers initially concluded that the reason for the high rate of burnout was pervasive pastoral fatigue. Pastors were being expected to work long hours to serve declining congregations with diminishing finances, weakening denominational commitments, lower biblical literacy, and smaller staffs. The pressures were obviously creating unbearable workloads for each pastor who had intended to serve God through a life of meditation within a sedate congregation at "the little brown church in the dell."

While it made good sense that increasing demands on pastors' families, finances, and energies were responsible for so many pastors leaving ministry, further research failed to confirm that conclusion. While there certainly were pastors who expected ministry to be sweet, few believed it would be easy. Most entered the pastoral vocation with good energy, strong commitments, and few illusions about finding a church with a white picket fence that kept out all difficult problems and people.

Fatigue was certainly a factor in pastoral burnout, but there was more to consider. More study revealed that workloads were not as damaging as "heartloads." The Moses factor that more and more preachers were facing was heavy workloads combined with a sense of being unappreciated for bearing them. It is one thing to feel the weight of the burdens of ministry, but quite another to be blamed for the burdens.

In Moses' case, he not only tires of a wilderness journey that had lasted almost half a century, he faces a congregation in rebellion—again. Adding to his weariness are people who do not merely complain, they blame. They quarrel with Moses and hound him with accusatory questions: "Why have you brought the assembly of the LORD into this wilderness, that we should die here, both we and our cattle?" and, "And why have you made us come up out of Egypt to bring us to this evil place?" The people attack the very leader who has sacrificed everything to save them. Their lack of support for him does more to exhaust his zeal for ministry than forty years of desert wandering.

IT'S NOT JUST FATIGUE THAT LEADS TO FAILURE

Good research over the last decade has disclosed that such factors are still at work in modern ministry. At the same time that pastors' workloads have been increasing, they are easy-target explanations for the diminishing congregations, finances, and loyalties. Local preachers are increasingly compared to the master communicators on radio and the internet. As lessening denominational loyalties lead to increased church shopping and hopping, ministers are too often judged for their "effectiveness" rather than their faithfulness. As pastoral respect diminishes throughout the culture for a variety of reasons, pastors and their families experience increased scrutiny and insecurity. Ministry seems increasingly dangerous, and ministers feel increasingly unappreciated.

These pressures with other contributing factors can lead many preachers to feel the pain expressed by a pastor friend of mine when he says, "I feel guilty when I sit down." Such intractable pressure (real or perceived) does not merely result in fatigue but in resentment that feeds a brooding anger that is far more debilitating that tiredness alone.

Fatigue, though it can destroy, more often only drains our stamina and sets up the heart for the Moses factor that is defined by a combination of tiredness *and* anger. Tiredness is not usually a sufficient cause for preachers to conclude that they must leave ministry but, if you combine fatigue with anger, then energy for, and commitment to, pastoral tasks and sacrifices drain quickly. We can shoulder extremely heavy loads imposed by others until our hearts begin to whisper, "How dare they?"

We will sacrifice for others with incredible stamina and selflessness until we begin to wonder why others do not sacrifice for us. We can minister much to others out of appreciation for Christ until we find ourselves thinking more about how much others do not appreciate us.

PASSING THE HEART TEST

No one will be able to take from the shoulders of responsible pastors the heavy loads of ministry. But Rick Reed writes from pastoral experience and leadership to help us understand what will *test* the pastoral heart and what God provides to *strengthen* it. Pastors who are willing to look clearly and unflinchingly into the challenges for continued ministry that reside in their own hearts will find *The Heart of the Preacher* invaluable and re-invigorating for ministry.

We need such a book because feeling isolated, overworked, and unappreciated in ministry at the same time we are fearing failure, embarrassment, and conflict is the Moses factor that is not confined to ancient history. Even as I write these words, I become aware that these warnings and observations from me are, more frequently than I wish, needed by me.

I know the pain of personal attack, the pressure to succeed, and the disappointment of not meeting others' expectations. I know how bitterness can grow in me when complaints about me multiply in others. I know that, in order to continue to minister, I need the counsel of a man of God like Rick Reed who loves the ministry, loves God's people, and loves the Savior. In *The Heart of the Preacher*, my friend Rick demonstrates that these loves are strong in his heart, and provides insights to sustain them in ours, so that we may minister with integrity and longevity for the glory of our Savior and the good of his people.

Bryan Chapell,
Pastor, Grace Presbyterian Church
President emeritus, Covenant Seminary

INTRODUCTION

Preaching is hard work. Anyone who tells you otherwise either has the gifting of Charles Spurgeon (highly unlikely) or is not doing biblical preaching. Practically everyone who takes up the joyful burden of preaching God's Word discovers that effective sermons don't come about easily or automatically.

When I was getting started as a preacher, the fact that preaching requires hard work didn't come as a major shock. My big surprise came when I realized the hardest work a preacher must do happens within the preacher's own heart. Over time, I've found the most challenging part of a sustained preaching ministry is not the rigor required to exegete a text, the thinking needed to discern the main message, the skill involved in crafting a clear and compelling outline, or even the energy necessary to communicate with authentic passion. My biggest challenge is keeping my heart in good order week in and week out. Preaching is not just hard work; it's *heart* work.

In speaking of preaching as heart work, I'm using the term "heart" as understood in Scripture. While current cultural usage treats "heart" as a synonym for emotions, the Bible presents a far more robust, holistic viewpoint. In Scripture, "heart" refers to "the center or focus of man's inner personal life."[1] As Tim Keller points out, while the heart produces emotions, it also thinks, wills, plans, decides, and trusts.[2] Preaching has a way of testing this part of those who engage in it regularly.

TESTS OF THE HEART

I had the privilege of attending a seminary with a history of training excellent expositors. My professors taught me the importance of exegesis, hermeneutics, big ideas, clarity, and application. What was harder to learn in a homiletics class was how life and ministry would test my heart.

When I started in pastoral ministry, its pressures and demands tempted me to skim the text, rather than soak in it, as I prepared to preach. Prioritizing and protecting time for sermon preparation turned out to be less of a time-management problem and more of a self-control challenge.

I would carve out time to prepare my sermons, but I inevitably faced another test: Would I allow the text to determine the

---

1. O. R. Brandon, "Heart," in *Evangelical Dictionary of Theology,* ed. Walter A. Elwell (Grand Rapids: Baker, 1984), 499.

2. Timothy Keller, *Preaching* (New York: Penguin Random House, 2015), 158.

substance of my sermon, or would I use the text to support my thoughts? Would I follow the terrain of the text wherever it led, or would I chart my own sermonic path, making the text head in a direction of my choosing?

Beyond these challenges, though, a host of unseen battles began to wage war inside my heart. On Sundays when the sermon went well, my heart overflowed with relief, gratitude, and joy. Then, without warning, pride would start to seep in and muddy the waters of my heart. On the Sundays when my sermon fell flat, I too felt flattened. I had to fight the urge to withdraw and become self-focused. In the lobby after the service or on the drive home, I fished for words of affirmation to bolster my sagging spirit.

The tests didn't stop there. Attending a gathering of pastors or hearing of friends serving in high-profile ministries often triggered competitive urges, unwanted feelings of comparison, or a deflating sense of insignificance.

Ministry turbulence and relational tensions brought still more tests for my heart. How do you speak with confidence when you've been shaken by conflict? How do you preach well when all is not well with your own soul? How do you proclaim the goodness of God when you are not in a good place? Who can you even talk to about these matters?

The way we handle these tests of the heart will affect how we hold up in ministry. Most preachers have friends from seminary who did not last in ministry in spite of being unusually bright students, incredibly insightful exegetes, and remarkably gifted communicators. They didn't lack aptitude or ability; they had a heart problem. In some cases, their hearts gave way to sinful attitudes and actions. In other cases, their hearts gave up from being worn down and hardened by the sins of others.

THE HEART OF A PREACHER

These challenges launched me on a journey into the heart of the preacher. I went back to God's Word for correction and direction; I also listened to wise counsel from seasoned, godly preachers—some I knew personally and others I only knew through their writings.

In this book, I seek to pass along the heart-level lessons God has been teaching me over the past thirty-plus years of preaching. I've had the chance to test these findings with other pastors and with the students I teach in homiletics courses at Heritage College and Seminary. My heart in writing is to help *your* heart as a preacher.

The book is organized into two parts. In the first, *The Testing of a Preacher's Heart*, I highlight fifteen heart-level tests preachers often experience as they seek to preach God's Word. These tests—such as dealing with ambition, comparison, or insignificance—are commonly faced but not commonly addressed in preaching books or at pastoral gatherings.

Part II, *The Strengthening of a Preacher's Heart,* provides practical guidance intended to help preachers prepare their hearts to face these heart tests in God-honoring, soul-stabilizing ways. While we cannot keep our hearts from being tested, we can take intentional steps to get ready for the tests. Each of the final ten chapters deals with a habit God has used to strengthen my soul to better proclaim his Word.

The hardest part of preaching is the heart work it requires. If you have a passion to preach and teach God's Word, I invite you to join me on this journey into the heart of a preacher.

PART I
THE TESTING OF A PREACHER'S HEART

The crucible is for silver and the furnace
for gold, but the LORD tests the heart.

Proverbs 17:3

Preach for any length of time, and you'll come to understand the truth of this verse in a very personal way. The Lord does indeed test the hearts of his preachers. And he often uses the crucible of a preaching ministry to do it.

When the heat gets turned up in ministry, the impurities within our hearts tend to bubble up to the surface. Scalding words of criticism melt us down, testing internal security and emotional resilience. Warm words of praise build us up but also test our humility. And that's just the beginning.

God's agenda in testing our hearts is not just to expose what's in them. He already knows that perfectly. His larger purpose goes beyond *revealing* to *refining*. He works through the fiery tests that scorch and soften our hearts to reshape us from the inside out. He plans to purify our faith and burnish our character. He molds and makes us into preachers who can better reflect his glory through our lives and our preaching.

In part I, I highlight fifteen heart-level tests I've faced over the years. While there are undoubtedly more than fifteen ways in which a preacher's heart may be tested, each of these has had a shaping effect on my soul—both as a person and a preacher. As you read and reflect on them, I hope you will recognize God's heart-level work in your own life and ministry.

1
AMBITION

One of my favorite preacher jokes would be a lot funnier if it weren't so convicting.

A pastor and his wife were driving home after the morning service. "Do you know what Mrs. Peterson told me today? She said I was one of the great expositors of our time." His wife remained quiet, eyes straight ahead. After a few moments of silence, he continued, "I wonder how many great expositors there are in our day?" Without a pause, she answered: "I don't know. But there's one less than you think."

Most of us aren't likely to be named one of the great expositors of our time. But that doesn't mean we wouldn't appreciate being nominated. Like the pastor in the joke, we can have our own secret exposition ambitions. Some days we daydream of greatness. Even if we can't be a legend in our own time, we can at least be a legend in our own minds. Even if we aren't one of the great expositors of our day, there will be days when our hearts are tested by the pull of ambition.

AMBITION SUSPICION

Ambition is defined as the strong desire to achieve something. This is a tricky topic for us as preachers, as ambition can be godly or fleshly. Strong ambition can drive us to improve, but it can also drive us crazy.

Godly ambition can fuel a passion to proclaim Christ to people who have yet to hear the gospel. This worked for the apostle Paul: "I make it my ambition to preach the gospel, not where Christ has already been named" (Romans 15:20). But where godly ambition motivates us to preach the message, fleshly ambition messes with our motives. We end up preaching for the wrong reasons.

Godly ambition turns fleshly when it becomes selfish ambition—something the Bible repeatedly condemns: "Do nothing from selfish ambition or conceit" (Philippians 2:3). God knows that when ambition turns selfish, ministry turns sour: "For where jealousy and selfish ambition exist, there will be disorder and every vile practice" (James 3:16).

A challenge we face as preachers comes in discerning whether our ambition is God-honoring or self-promoting. Honest, accurate assessment is complicated by our vulnerability to self-deception in matters of the heart. We tend to assume the best about ourselves and overlook the worst.

CHASING AMBITION

Ever hear the name Salmon P. Chase? You may be familiar with Chase bank, a financial institution that bears his name. His story is woven into historian Doris Kearns Goodwin's best seller *Team of Rivals*.

Chase ran unsuccessfully against Abraham Lincoln in the Republican primary of 1860. Still, Lincoln selected Chase as his Secretary of the Treasury, considering him the best man for the job. Unfortunately, Chase continued to believe he was the best man for Lincoln's job. He remained ambitious to replace Lincoln even while serving in his cabinet, undercutting him to prop up his chances of replacing him.

While this kind of maneuvering is rather common in political circles, two aspects of Chase's ambition caught my attention in a way that hit closer to home. First, Chase was a churchgoing, Bible-believing, morally upright man. He read Scripture and prayed daily. He faithfully attended an evangelical church. In many ways, he qualified as one of the "good guys."

Second, Chase somehow remained clueless about his own selfish ambition. In his journals and letters, he repeatedly casts his actions in noble, virtuous terms. He was convinced that he sought the good of the nation while he ardently pursued his own selfish ends. Sadly, he could never seem to smell the foul odor of his own selfish ambition, but everyone else could.

As Goodwin notes, "Chase could not separate his own ambition from the cause he championed. The most calculating decisions designed to forward his political career were justified by advancement of the cause."[1] Or in the words of historian Stephen Mazlish, "Chase could join his passion for personal advancement to the demands of his religious convictions. ... 'Fame's proud temple' could be his and he need feel no guilt in its pursuit."[2]

Chase's life serves as a cautionary tale for preachers: selfish ambition can infect the heart of those who show signs of genuine spiritual life. We can remain in the dark about the dark side of our own ambition. It's dangerously easy to convince ourselves we are pursuing Christ's glory while advancing our own selfish ends.

REDEEMING AMBITION

So what should a preacher do to guard against selfish ambition? Some might argue the safest course of action involves the total abolition of ambition. But Paul shows us a better way.

From candid comments recorded in his letters, we get the sense that Paul was naturally ambitious. As a young man, he desired to excel. He understood his personal trajectory as headed upward toward prominence. As he wrote to the Galatians, "I was advancing in Judaism beyond many of my own age among my people, so extremely zealous was I for the

---

1. Doris Kearns Goodwin, *Team of Rivals: The Political Genius of Abraham Lincoln* (New York: Simon and Schuster, 2005), 109.

2. Stephen Mazlish, quoted in Goodwin, *Team of Rivals,* 109.

traditions of my fathers" (Galatians 1:14). Like Salmon Chase, Paul blended his personal ambition with his spiritual commitments. He sought to make a difference for his cause and make a name for himself.

Being captured and captivated by Christ brought a radical change to Paul's life, including a change to his ambitions. Paul didn't discard his desire to make a difference. Neither did he lose his drive or tireless work ethic (1 Corinthians 15:9–10: "I worked harder than all of them"). Instead, he lost his need to promote himself or impress other people. His selfish ambition took a big hit.

We see the change in Paul's ambition when the Christians in Corinth put him in an awkward situation. The believers in the church in Corinth had a nasty tendency to rank ministers and promote their favorite (1 Corinthians 1:12). While some preferred Paul, others were big fans of Apollos (a capable, captivating preacher, Acts 18:24–28) or Peter (the recognized leader of the apostles).

Paul could have easily felt threatened and insecure. Fleshly ambition could have driven him toward self-promotion or ministerial competition. But Paul would have none of it. His response to the Corinthians reveals how Christ had supernaturally reoriented his natural ambition. In 1 Corinthians 4:1–5, Paul highlights four truths that, if we hold on to them, will keep us from drifting toward selfish ambition.

We are servants and stewards—not celebrities. "This is how one should regard us, as servants of Christ and stewards of the mysteries of God" (4:1). Paul saw himself as a servant of Christ and a steward of his message; he encouraged others to view him that way as well. He fought against the tendency to turn ministers into celebrities. To combat fleshly ambition, I must consciously adopt the identity of a servant and steward, resisting the dark desire to be seen as a semi-celebrity.

We must test our own hearts, but not fully trust our own tests. "I am not aware of anything against myself, but I am not thereby acquitted" (4:4). Paul understood that self-examination was essential for a minister. We should test the motives of our hearts and seek to live with a clear conscience. But, like Paul, we must remember our own assessment isn't foolproof. Our self-appraisals may not be fully accurate. We may fail to detect the odor of selfish ambition that others can smell, so we need to make a habit of listening to others' evaluations of our actions.

Christ will evaluate our motives and not just our actions. "It is the Lord who judges me. Therefore do not pronounce judgment before the time, before the Lord comes, who will bring to light the things now hidden in darkness and will disclose the purposes of the heart" (4:4b–5a). Paul envisioned a day when Christ would evaluate the hidden purposes of his heart. He knew that Christ knew his motives. He might be able to fool others, or even fool himself; however, he could never fool the Lord Jesus. This truth sobers me and moves me to intentionally invite the Lord to search my heart and know my thoughts (Psalm 139:23). I don't want to be painfully surprised on judgment day.

God will commend us for faithful ministry. "Then each one will receive his commendation from God" (4:5b). We should be sobered by the thought of Christ doing an audit of our ministry motives. However, we don't have to be terrified. Paul makes it clear that God's desire is to find something in us to commend! In his eyes, faithfulness is success: "Moreover, it is required of stewards that they be found faithful" (4:2). As we seek to faithfully serve Christ and regularly bring our hearts into the light of his presence, we can anticipate his commendation on the final day.

This side of heaven, we will always need God's supervision over our ambition. Our motives will become mixed at times. We will need to regularly allow God's Spirit to redeem and reorder our ambition as preachers. Still, we can serve with a sense of anticipation and joy. The Lord Jesus redeemed Paul's natural ambition, and he can do the same in us.

2
COMPARISON

Imagine you've just finished giving your best effort preaching the parable of the prodigal son from Luke 15. One well-meaning parishioner rushes to meet you after the service ends and says, "Pastor, have you heard Tim Keller's message on this passage? It's awesome. I'll send you the link." He makes no comment about your message or its impact. He just goes on and on about Keller's sermon.

Later that afternoon, you still find yourself somewhat deflated by the conversation. It's not that you don't appreciate Keller's ministry. You honestly do. But you don't appreciate having your sermon compared to his—especially when it's clear your message didn't measure up. You think of witty replies your unsanctified self would have loved to make: "Why don't we just play Tim Keller's sermons on Sunday mornings at church so people can really be fed well?" Or "Next time you are in the hospital, why don't you call Tim's office and see if he will stop by for a pastoral visit?"

Even after fending off your fleshly responses, you still feel disappointed with yourself: "Why does this bother me so much? Why am I so insecure? Why can't I rejoice that God used Tim's sermon to shape the spiritual life of someone in my congregation?" This is what comparison does.

COMPARISON CATEGORIES

As I've reflected on my own battle with comparison, I've realized this heart test comes to us as preachers in at least four different ways.

Comparing abilities. According to Romans 12:7, teaching makes the list of spiritual gifts used to strengthen the church. While God uniquely gifts some to be pastors and teachers (Ephesians 4:11), he doesn't gift them uniformly. Abilities vary. What's more, even Spirit-given giftings must be developed.

Having been a homiletics professor for years, I have seen how teaching gifts can be developed through insight, effort, and experience. However, even when students work equally hard, they don't preach equally well. Some have greater capabilities when it comes to effectively exegeting and expositing a text of Scripture.

Preachers recognize excellence when we hear it in another's sermon. As we listen to an exceptionally gifted expositor, we can feel simultaneously impressed and diminished. On the one hand, we admire his ability to preach so well, the same way we would a piano virtuoso playing a Bach concerto or a Cy Young-winning pitcher painting the corners of home plate. We know he's worked hard to do what he does. We also know that no amount of hard work would allow us to duplicate his efforts.

Most of us don't aspire to become a concert pianist or to pitch for the Yankees. However, we do want to be effective preachers. So while we don't compare ourselves to great pianists or pitchers, we sometimes do with great preachers. And the comparison doesn't usually flatter us.

Comparing opportunities. Like spiritual gifts, ministry opportunities aren't distributed equally among God's servants. Jesus' parable of the laborers in the vineyard (Matthew 20:1–16) has some working a full day, some a half of a day, and some only an hour. At quitting time, the Master pays them equally. Until pay time, the last group of workers may have felt rather short-changed by life. They had been overlooked, left on the sidelines while others were given opportunity and responsibility.

Preachers sometimes feel that way as we evaluate the ministry opportunities we've been given compared to those of others. We have friends from seminary who serve congregations that are impressive in size or standing. We watch others receive invitations to preach at denominational gatherings or high-profile conferences. We can see ourselves as one of the workers relegated to stand on the sidelines watching others step into amazing opportunities.

Comparing impact. While we know the full effect of our preaching will not be known until heaven, we long to see evidence of impact here on earth. We ask God to use our sermons to bring people to salvation and greater sanctification. When we hear God is working powerfully through the sermons of others, we can sometimes struggle with comparison. Why isn't God working that way through us?

Comparing perks. This category is awkward to mention. After all, preachers are servants of Christ, not divas. We didn't go into ministry for fame or money. But that doesn't mean we don't notice the material blessings some preachers enjoy: the make or model of their cars; the size and style of their homes; their seemingly unlimited expense accounts for books and conferences. We know this kind of comparison is fleshly, but our flesh still compares.

THE COMPARISON CONUNDRUM

So what's a preacher to do? What does the Bible say about comparison and how we should handle it in a godly way? I see Scripture giving two appropriate but contrasting responses: kill it quickly and use it wisely.

Kill it quickly. While you won't find comparison mentioned in the "works of the flesh" in Galatians 5:19–21, comparison is a close relative of several characteristics that make the list:

jealousy, rivalry, and envy. Comparison also shares the same spiritual DNA as selfish ambition.

While I hate to admit it, my tendency to compare myself with others is often fueled by a high-octane, competitive spirit. That makes comparison a refined byproduct of pride. C. S. Lewis explains the connection between competition and pride in his book *Mere Christianity*:

> Pride is essentially competitive—is competitive by its very nature—while the other vices are competitive only, so to speak, by accident. Pride gets no pleasure out of having something, only out of having more of it than the next man. We say that people are proud of being rich, or clever, or good-looking, but they are not. They are proud of being richer, or cleverer, or better looking than others. ... Once the element of competition has gone, pride has gone.[1]

The comparison that grows from the root of pride is sinful and deadly. Scripture speaks clearly on what we should do with sinful attitudes and actions: put them to death through the power of God's Spirit. Listen to Romans 8:13: "For if you live according to the flesh you will die, but if by the Spirit you put to death the deeds of the body, you will live." Paul's language sounds stark, even grisly. Sin must not find sanctuary to live as a fugitive in our souls. This is a matter of spiritual life or death.

---

1. C. S. Lewis, *Mere Christianity* (New York: HarperCollins, 2001), 122.

As the seventeenth-century Puritan John Owen put it, "Be killing sin or it will be killing you."[2]

So when I notice comparison pushing its way into my thinking, stirring up my competitive juices and selfish ambition, I must quickly hand it over to the Spirit to be killed. "Lord," I whisper, "I hate this struggle with my competitive comparisons toward another servant of yours. I confess this as sin and ask you, by the power of your Spirit, to help me put it to death. Thank you for your grace that both convicts and cleanses."

Use it wisely. Because of comparison's close ties to selfish ambition and pride, we might conclude it is unredeemable, always and only sinful. But surprisingly, Scripture teaches otherwise. In fact, comparison has a legitimate role in the life of a minister—if we use it wisely.

Read through the New Testament and you'll discover Paul sometimes used comparison to assess himself and others. He benchmarked his work ethic against other ministers and concluded, "I worked harder than any of them, though it was not I, but the grace of God that is with me" (1 Corinthians 15:10). While Paul gauged his level of effort, in part by comparing himself to others in ministry, he intentionally fought against pride by crediting God's grace for his efforts and accomplishments.

Comparison can sometimes aid us in our own efforts at self-assessment. While the primary standard for life and ministry

---

2. John Owen, *On the Mortification of Sin in Believers,* The Works of John Owen 6 (Edinburgh: T&T Clark, 1862), 9.

must be God's Word, we can benefit from looking at our lives in light of other committed servants of Christ. Over the years, I've been greatly challenged by reading biographies of Christian leaders from previous eras—Charles Spurgeon, George Müller, or Dietrich Bonhoeffer. Comparing my commitment and devotion with theirs spurs me to pursue further growth.

When done wisely, comparison not only helps us evaluate ourselves, it also assists us in assessing others. For example, Paul compared Timothy to other ministers and ranked Timothy at the top of his list: "For I have no one like him, who will be genuinely concerned for your welfare" (Philippians 2:20). This kind of comparison is an essential part of making wise leadership decisions. When done realistically and charitably, comparison allows leaders to assign the right people to the right positions.

There is still another way comparison proves spiritually useful for ministers. Here again, we learn from Paul. He constantly compared the sufferings he experienced while serving Christ with the glories that awaited him in heaven. "For this light momentary affliction is preparing for us an eternal weight of glory beyond all comparison, as we look not to the things that are seen but to the things that are unseen. For the things that are seen are transient, but the things that are unseen are eternal" (2 Corinthians 4:17–18). When Paul put earthly hardships next to eternal glories, there was no comparison.

COMPARISON CHOLESTEROL

In a way, comparison functions a bit like cholesterol. We can't live without cholesterol in our bloodstreams; that's why our bodies naturally produce it. However, the wrong kind of cholesterol elevates our risk of heart disease.

Like cholesterol, comparison is both necessary and potentially deadly. When done in the wrong way, it raises our risk of spiritual heart disease. However, under the Spirit's control, comparison can help us assess ourselves and assign responsibilities to others.

So while irritating and insensitive, the guy who rushes up after Sunday's sermon to gush about another preacher's message may be doing us a favor. Unwittingly, he is forcing us to face ourselves—to see the sanctifying work remaining to be done in our hearts. As we embrace the upside of God refining our character, the painful comment that triggered it pales by comparison.

3
BOASTING

When it comes to gauging our abilities as preachers, most of us don't follow the lead of British soccer manager, Brian Clough. When a reporter asked Clough to assess his performance as a coach, he replied, "I wouldn't say I'm the best manager in the business, but I'm in the top one."[1]

Preachers generally go to the opposite extreme. When conversing about our capabilities as preachers, we gravitate toward self-deprecation much more than self-promotion. In the dictionary, "boast" may be a five-letter word; however, in our ministry lexicons, we classify it as a foul, four-letter word.

1. Robert Philip, "Brian Clough's Words and Deeds Still Stand Out," *The Telegraph,* March 21, 2008, www.telegraph.co.uk/sport/football/2295033/Brian -Cloughs-words-and-deeds-still-stand-out.html.

In spite of our distaste for boasting in its flagrant forms, boasting is still one of the tests we face as preachers, since we can easily succumb to a more subtle version of this vice. The Greek term for boasting (*kauchaomai*) carries the sense of "glorying." To glory means to revel in, to feel elevated or lifted up by something or someone. As such, boasting can happen covertly, in the privacy of our own hearts and minds. Boasting includes not just the talking we do about ourselves, but also our self-talk— our inward ruminations and rejoicings. As such, boasting is a bigger problem than we often realize.

Paul exposed this boasting problem in a group of ministers who had gained influence among the Christians in Galatia. These Jewish ministry leaders—often labeled as Judaizers— promoted circumcision as a spiritual requirement for all Gentile believers. In his Letter to the Galatians, Paul not only rejected their theological reasoning, he also rebuked them for their boasting.

> It is those who want to make a good showing in the flesh who would force you to be circumcised, and only in order that they may not be persecuted for the cross of Christ. For even those who are circumcised do not themselves keep the law, but they desire to have you circumcised that they may boast in your flesh. (Galatians 6:12–13)

The phrase "boast in your flesh" sounds rather strange to our ears. Who, we wonder, would gain their sense of significance from signing people up for circumcision? The answer comes when we remember circumcision served as a sign of allegiance to the entire Mosaic law. So getting more Gentiles circumcised meant more ministry influence for these Jewish leaders. Circumcision equaled success. And success provided a reason for boasting.

As preachers, we certainly don't measure success in terms of circumcisions. However, we still have our ways of measuring. Whether our metrics are Sunday attendance numbers, sermon podcast downloads, or outside speaking invitations, we can fall into the trap of boasting about our ministry influence—even if we only do it silently, within our hearts.

NO MORE BOASTING— WITH ONE EXCEPTION

Paul rejected the whole notion of boasting about ministry influence, though he could have easily played that game. After all, he had brought the gospel to this region and successfully planted the church. He could have gloried in the impact of his preaching ministry among the Galatians. But he rejected ministry success as a reason for boasting. In fact, he went further; he rejected all boasting—with one notable exception. "But far be it from me to boast except in the cross of our Lord Jesus Christ, by which the world has been crucified to me, and I to the world" (Galatians 6:14).

The cross had a lethal effect on Paul's tendency to boast in his accomplishments. Before he met Christ, Paul viewed spiritual service as a means to personal advancement. As he confessed to the Galatians, "And I was advancing in Judaism beyond many of my own age among my people, so extremely zealous was I for the traditions of my fathers" (Galatians 1:14). Paul was keeping score. He compared himself to others his age and liked what he saw. Like Brian Clough, he ranked himself "in the top one." But when Christ called him to salvation, everything changed. Something died—Paul's penchant for boasting in himself, his reputation, and ministry success. Now he could only boast in the cross.

THE SCANDAL OF BOASTING IN THE CROSS

Like Paul, by God's grace we've come to understand the mystery and message of the cross. We have embraced the cross personally and preach it publicly. Boasting in the cross makes perfect sense to us. What we sometimes forget is that boasting in the cross made no sense to people in Paul's day. His words would have sounded like nonsense to both Gentiles and Jews.

Gentiles would never boast in the cross. In fact, they didn't even like to talk about the cross. Cicero, a Roman historian and statesman, wrote: "Not only let the cross be absent from the person of Roman citizens, but its very name from their thoughts, eyes and ears."[2] The Latin word for cross (*crux*)—which gives us our English word excruciating—was a word you didn't say in polite company. Instead, you euphemistically spoke of the "unlucky tree." Boasting in the cross seemed as revolting to most Gentiles as boasting in beheadings seems to us.

---

2. Quoted in Mourant Brock, *The Cross: Heathen and Christian*, 3rd ed. (London: Elliot Stock, 1882), 50.

If Gentiles didn't boast in the cross, Jews were even less likely to do so. After all, the Mosaic law made it clear that "a hanged man is cursed by God" (Deuteronomy 21:23). If Gentiles saw crucifixion as being cursed by the state, Jews saw it as being cursed by God. Who would boast about that?

Paul shared the worldview of those who saw crucifixion as being cursed by God. That's precisely why he boasted "in the cross of our Lord Jesus Christ." As he had already explained to the Galatians, Jesus went to the cross knowing it meant coming under God's curse: "Christ redeemed us from the curse of the law by becoming a curse for us—for it is written, 'Cursed is everyone who is hanged on a tree'" (Galatians 3:13). As unthinkable as it sounds, the sinless Son of God willingly chose to experience the curse of God's white-hot judgment against sin.

But there's more. Not only did Christ put himself under God's curse, he did it for us and in our place. We broke God's laws and his heart. We rightfully deserved God's curse: "Cursed be everyone who does not abide by all things written in the Book of the Law, and do them" (Galatians 3:10). Paul knew the cross of Christ had his name on it.

As Paul came to grasp the meaning and message of the cross, it killed his natural tendency to glory in himself and his accomplishments. The cross of Christ became the means "by which the world has been crucified to me, and I to the world" (Galatians 6:14). Worldly standards of success lost their power over him. He dropped out of the race to be "in the top one." For Paul, the cross of Christ killed all other reasons for boasting.

PUTTING BOASTING IN ITS PLACE

How should Paul's exhortation and example shape us as preachers? It should help us put boasting in its proper place. We should consciously and continuously focus our hearts on what Christ accomplished for us by his substitutionary death on the cross. Like Paul, we must let the cross have a lethal impact on our innate tendency to glory in our ministry impact. Our hearts should regularly sing, "I will not boast in anything, no gifts, no power, no wisdom; but I will boast in Jesus Christ, his death and resurrection."[3]

Does this mean that preachers should no longer care about their ministry impact or spiritual influence? Should we be indifferent to how people respond to our preaching, deflecting their appreciation and dismissing their affection? Not at all. Paul rejoiced to see the Galatians changed by his gospel preaching and their concern for his welfare (Galatians 4:14–15). However, something had shifted inside Paul's heart. He no longer gloried in his accomplishments for Christ, but in what Christ had accomplished for him on the cross.

So what should we do when our hearts and minds revert to old ways of glorying in ourselves, our personal influence, or our ministry impact? As soon as God's Spirit convicts of us of an inward glory shift, we should respond in two ways: squash and survey.

---

3. Stuart Townend, "How Deep the Father's Love for Us" (Thankyou Music, 1995), www.stuarttownend.co.uk/song/how-deep-the-fathers-love-for-us.

Squash signifies crushing self-glory, like a bug under your shoe. We put sin to death by the power of the Spirit (Romans 8:13). We confess the pull to self-glory, asking God for grace and forgiveness. As I spiritually squash the temptation to bogus boasting, I've sometimes found it helpful to physically stamp my foot, as if smashing a poisonous spider.

Survey speaks of refocusing attention on Christ and his cross. "Survey" calls us to remember the good news of the gospel message—Christ died on the cross to redeem us from the curse, forgive our sins (including self-glory), and give us new life as part of his church. The best way to get our eyes off ourselves and our desire for self-glory is to refocus them on Christ. As Isaac Watts put it so beautifully in his hymn: "When I survey the wondrous cross on which the prince of glory died, my richest gain I count but loss and pour contempt on all my pride."

The more we glory in the cross, the deeper we will understand what Paul discovered: the cross of Christ kills all other reasons for boasting.

4
INSIGNIFICANCE

A well-known Christian preacher tells the story of driving to speak at a church, his two young children riding in the backseat. When they arrived, the parking lot was almost empty—only three other cars. His son looked out the window and said, "Dad, nobody's coming to hear you. And you're so famous." His daughter turned to her brother and said, "Well, if Dad's so famous, where are all the people?" Feeling defensive for his dad, the boy shot back, "Knock it off. It's hard to be famous when nobody knows who you are."

That boy was right: *It's hard to be famous when no one knows who you are.*

A pastor friend once sent me an email suggesting several possible speakers for the annual preaching lectures we host at Heritage Seminary. He recommended several heavy-hitters in the homiletics world. He closed his note by saying if we couldn't get any of them to come, he was available. The only problem, he added, was we'd have to charge $1,000 per ticket to make up for the fact that only four or five people would show up to hear him—one of whom would be his mother.

His note made me smile. It also made me reflect. My friend voiced what many pastors feel. We're not about to receive an invitation to headline a conference anytime soon. If we did, there would only be three cars in the parking lot and one of the cars would belong to Mom.

It's hard to be famous when no one knows who you are.

IN GOOD COMPANY

Most pastors will always be relatively unknown. We may serve a city church lost in a larger metropolis. We may serve a rural church located on the outskirts of obscurity. Sure, we'll be known to the people in our congregations. But beyond that—not so much. Our sermons may be on our church website, but they won't go viral.

Most of the time, that's just fine. Most of the time, when busy serving Christ and his people, we don't think too much about it. We enjoy our calling and find satisfaction in serving. Besides, we went into ministry to be faithful, not famous.

But sometimes, unexpectedly, something will surface our latent insecurity: hearing about the exponential growth happening at a friend's church or reading an article by a seminary friend who now leads a high-profile ministry. We can feel diminished by a comment made at a pastors' lunch, or even the well-meaning words of one of our kids in the backseat. As we compare ourselves with others or with our own unspoken hopes and dreams, we suddenly feel small and unimportant. We find ourselves facing the heart test of insignificance.

The New Testament has a message for all of us who sometimes struggle with a sense of insignificance. It reminds us we are in good company. When Paul wrote the believers in Corinth, he described himself and his colleagues as "unknown, and yet well known" (2 Corinthians 6:9).

We know Paul as one of the high-profile Christian leaders of the early church. If someone carved a Mount Rushmore for Christian ministers, we'd vote for Paul's face to be on it. He seems larger than life.

Still, Paul had a realistic understanding of his place in society. He knew he was relatively unknown in the larger Roman world. He may have been "known" among the fledgling churches, but he could still classify himself as one of the "unknowns" in the wider culture.

But being an unknown in the world didn't rob Paul of joy or diminish his contentment in ministry. What mattered most to him was being known by the One who mattered most. By grace, he had come to know God and be known by him (Galatians 4:9). As a result, he lived with a sense of significance anchored in the eternal. Paul learned to find his significance in being well-known to Jesus. God wants us to learn that same life-giving lesson.

In my first experience as a lead pastor, part of God's gracious curriculum for me involved reorienting my sense of significance. I served as the solo pastor of a West Coast church with an unpaved parking lot and an unusual, L-shaped sanctuary. The people in the congregation loved me and my family, and we felt grateful for the privilege of serving a healthy congregation. At least most of the time.

There were moments when I struggled with a sense of insignificance. In seminary, I had dreams of doing great things for God, of being a missionary and equipping people to reach an entire nation. My wife had been trained as a Bible translator. But we found ourselves tucked away in a small church, in a small town that seemed miles away from our earlier hopes and dreams.

MISSIONARIES AND A MOVIE

God used some missionaries and a movie to begin reshaping my internal sense of significance. First, I heard about a missionary couple serving Christ on the Mosquito Coast of Honduras. This family had labored in obscurity there for twenty or thirty years. Talk about being "unknown." But from what I heard, it didn't seem to bother them.

Next, Linda and I had the opportunity to visit missionary friends in Indonesia. For several weeks we lived with men and women who prayed and planned to impact an entire nation with the gospel. While inspired by their vision, I felt dwarfed in comparison. My life and ministry seemed so small and insignificant.

Shortly after returning home, my wife and I went to see a newly released movie, *Mr. Holland's Opus*. If you've seen the movie, you know it tells the story of a man who dreamed of composing a beautiful symphony, his magnum opus. It would be his lasting musical legacy. But life didn't go the way he planned. Instead of becoming a famous conductor, he became a high school music teacher. It was not exactly his dream job, but it paid the bills. The years rolled by quickly; soon Mr. Holland was an older man being pushed into retirement as the district head office cut funding for music programs. As he cleaned out his desk and made a final walk down the hallway into retirement, a student asked him to step into the school auditorium. To his surprise, the seats were full of cheering people. On the stage sat former students ready to play a piece of music he had composed. One of the students honored him with the words, "Mr. Holland, we are your opus."

As I left the theater, my eyes brimmed with tears and my heart soared. I had been reminded that significance doesn't always come the way we expect or even want. In fact, the true measure of our work won't be seen until we walk the hallway into heaven's auditorium. Then, with heavenly hindsight, we'll see what we should have foreseen: faithfulness without fanfare makes us well-known to Jesus. Even if we spend our life serving in obscurity on the Mosquito Coast or in one of the many out-of-the-way places closer to home, we are famous in his eyes.

NO LITTLE PEOPLE

In his book *No Little People*, Francis Schaeffer writes, "As there are no little people in God's sight, so there are no little places. To be wholly committed to God in the place where God wants him—this is the creature glorified." Schaeffer goes further; he counsels that we not seek a bigger place "unless the Lord himself extrudes us into a greater one."[1] I don't recall ever reading the word "extrude" before, so I was thankful Schaeffer explained its meaning:

> The word extrude is important here. To be extruded is to be forced out under pressure into a desired shape. Picture a huge press jamming soft metal at high pressure through a die so that the metal comes out in a certain shape. This is the way of the Christian: He should choose the lesser place until God extrudes him into a position of more responsibility and authority.[2]

After serving a number of years as a pastor on the West Coast, I experienced what it's like to be extruded. In a way I could have never planned, God moved us to Ottawa, Canada, where I became the lead pastor at Metropolitan Bible Church. Pastoring this vibrant downtown congregation, filled with people from around the world (over forty languages spoken), was one of the great privileges and joys of my life. Then, after almost fifteen years at the Met, the Lord extruded me again—this time

---

1. Francis Schaeffer, *The Complete Works of Francis Schaeffer*, vol. 3 (Wheaton, IL: Crossway, 1982), 64.

2. Schaeffer, *Complete Works*, 64.

to train up a new generation of ministry leaders at Heritage College and Seminary.

What should we do on days when feelings of insignificance darken our outlook and diminish our joy? How should we respond when our hearts become restless and discontented with our ministry placement? We must preach to our own hearts. We must remind ourselves that it is too soon to know the significance of our service. Serving with passion and faithfulness is what God asks of us today. This is what makes a Christian well-known to Jesus. This is how we become, like Paul, a well-known unknown.

5
LAZINESS

"Must be nice to have a job where you only have to work one day a week."

Like many pastors, I've grimaced whenever I've heard someone make that statement, not knowing for sure if they were joking or not. But based on the pastors I've known over the years, the big challenge we face is exactly the opposite. Instead of only working one day a week, we struggle not to work all seven.

Over the course of my ministry, I've never been accused of being lazy. Like many pastors, I lean in the opposite direction— long hours, extra effort, continual motion. While some shirk when it comes to work, most in pastoral ministry live at a pace somewhere between busy and breathless.

But that doesn't mean busy pastors aren't lazy preachers. That's the convicting insight I gained when I first read Eugene Peterson's article "The Unbusy Pastor." Peterson contends that busy pastors can easily become lazy preachers. Like the lizards that slip into kings' palaces (Proverbs 30:28), laziness can slip into our lives as preachers. Especially when we get extremely busy in ministry.

Peterson links busyness to laziness in a surprising way:

> The ... reason I become busy is that I am lazy. I indolently let other people decide what I will do instead of resolutely deciding myself. I let people who do not understand the work of the pastor write the agenda for my day's work because I am too slipshod to write it myself. But these people don't know what a pastor is supposed to do. The pastor is a shadow figure in their minds, a marginal person vaguely connected with matters of God and good will. Anything remotely religious or somehow well-intentioned can be properly assigned to the pastor.[1]

He goes on to say this kind of lazy busyness or busy laziness keeps a pastor from becoming a faithful preacher. Busy pastors can become lazy preachers. As I've reflected on how laziness can creep into our lives as preachers, I've come to see laziness as more of a heart-level test than a time-management

---

1. Eugene Peterson, "The Unbusy Pastor," *CT Pastors*, 1981, www.christianity today.com/pastors/1981/summer/81l3070.html.

problem. I've also learned to spot five warning signs that I'm becoming a lazy preacher.

SCATTERING SERMON PREP TIME

The work of sermon preparation demands the best of our mental and spiritual energies. Compelling sermons demand clear thinking.

Paul made it clear to Timothy, and all preachers, that handling Scripture accurately would take our best efforts: "Do your best to present yourself to God as one approved, a worker who has no need to be ashamed, rightly handling the word of truth" (2 Timothy 2:15). The word translated "do your best" (*spoudazō*) has the idea of energy, effort, and diligence. The King James version reads, "Study to show yourself approved." That may not be the best translation of the text, but it's a fair application.

Our best efforts at studying Scripture don't happen on the fly, in the cracks, or when we are spent. We sabotage ourselves if we fail to block out time for study and writing when we are at our best.

The most effective remedy is to schedule sermon preparation time first. Block off study time that coincides with your peak level of alertness. For me, that means morning hours. I think one hour of study in the morning equals two or three in the afternoon, so I seek to study in the morning and schedule meetings and appointments for the afternoon. Establishing a regularly scheduled, extended block of devoted sermon prep time frees us from the exhausting dilemma of customizing each week. It also communicates to our congregations that preparing to proclaim God's Word to them is a high priority for us.

SQUANDERING SERMON PREP TIME

It's one thing to make time for sermon preparation; it's another thing to make the most of the time. Laziness shows up when we give way to distractions in the time set aside for sermon preparation. We check emails, send texts, or answer phone calls. We opt for easier tasks that don't demand the same level of focused concentration as sermon prep. We go easy on ourselves, pandering to our undisciplined fleshly desires.

The solution here is not difficult to identify; however, it's easier said than done. We need to exercise self-control. Paul knew that was to develop: "Urge the younger men to be self-controlled" (Titus 2:6). Middle-aged and older men need it too. Self-control keeps us from distracting ourselves when we are studying. We need to find a place where we won't be interrupted or put up a sign to signal we are unavailable. We must fight the urge to interrupt ourselves by checking emails, texts, favorite blogs, or news feeds. Self-discipline doesn't come naturally to most of us. Thankfully, it can come supernaturally; self-control is a spiritual fruit that ripens as we grow up in Christ (Galatians 5:22–23).

STARTING SERMON PREP TOO LATE

Sermons can be written at the last minute. There will be weeks when, due to crisis, illness, or travel, a pastor will need to produce a "Saturday night special." Still, most Saturday night specials aren't all that special.

Kenton Anderson says good sermons need to be slow-cooked, not microwaved. "Of course, as any decent chef will tell you, some things taste better when cooked slowly. Time can be a useful ingredient in deepening a rich and full-bodied taste. You don't always want to rush things in the kitchen. You don't always want to rush things in the pulpit."[2]

Slow cooking your sermons requires an early starting time. In my case, I blocked off significant time early in the week with the goal of having a draft manuscript completed by Wednesday afternoon. Later in the week I'd revisit my manuscript several times, making tweaks and revisions as needed.

When it comes to starting early on a sermon, I've benefitted from some advice from Haddon Robinson, who was for many years a professor of preaching at Gordon-Conwell Theological Seminary. He urged pastors to set aside an hour for studying a passage ten days before they would preach it. For example, if you were slated to preach Colossians 3:1–5 on February 21, you would spend one hour doing exegetical spadework in the passage on February 11. After one hour, you shut down your study on this passage. But, as Robinson explained, your mind will quietly continue to work on it. When you come back to the passage a few days later, you'll generally find you make progress more quickly.

---

2. Kenton C. Anderson, "Slow Cooking Sermons," *Preaching Today*, www.preachingtoday.com/skills/themes/structure/200104.26.html.

SKIMMING THE SURFACE
OF THE PASSAGE

Laziness also shows up when we don't take the time and effort to understand what the text is saying and preach what we want to say instead. This can happen when we come to a passage with a predetermined sense of what we want to preach from it. Then, as we actually begin to prepare the sermon, we discover there is more going on in the text than we originally understood. In fact, as we dig deeper into the passage, we come to the disquieting realization the text isn't emphasizing what we had planned to preach. However, we may have already turned in a sermon title to be printed in the bulletin or posted on the church website. The worship leaders may have already selected songs based on the direction we told them the sermon would take.

At this point, we face another test of our hearts. Will we do the hard work needed to understand the passage and preach what it says? Or will we simply use the biblical text as a starting point for the sermon we planned to preach? Eugene Peterson has the right pastoral instincts when he resists a superficial and skewed treatment of God's Word. He rejects the laziness that skims the surface of a passage rather than diving down deep: "I need a drenching in Scripture; I require an immersion in biblical studies. I need reflective hours over the pages of Scripture as well as personal struggles with the meaning of Scripture. That takes time, far more time than it takes to prepare a sermon."[3]

---

3. Peterson, "The Unbusy Pastor."

If we are going to preach God's Word faithfully, we must take the time needed to dig into the text and context of a passage; to wrestle with the author's flow of thought; to prayerfully reflect on the pastoral purpose of the passage; to let the sermon simmer in our souls. Pushing ourselves to start our exegetical work earlier allows us adequate time to understand the biblical author's message as well as unhurried time to pray the truth of the passage into our souls.

SERVING UP LEFTOVER SERMONS

Over the years, I've heard divergent views on whether preachers should ever reuse a sermon they've already preached. Some advocate starting from scratch every time. No reheating leftovers and serving them up again. Old sermons, like old manna, get moldy, they claim. Preaching leftover sermons is a sign of a lazy preacher.

While it's true that lazy preachers reheat sermons, repeating a sermon doesn't necessarily mean one is lazy. I've found that some sermons, like good lasagnes, actually set up better the second time they are served. Besides, when preaching in a different venue, an old sermon is new to a different audience.

But since it's easy for experienced preachers to over-rely on past sermons, we need to take precautions to prevent laziness from creeping in. I find it best to go over every line of the sermon manuscript, sharpening the flow of the message and updating illustrations and applications. While my general outline often stays relatively unchanged, changing illustrations and applications gives the sermon a fresh feel.

While there are times when we can heat up and re-serve a message, we should never stop preparing fresh sermons from scratch. In my role as a seminary president, I speak to a different congregation most weeks. For my heart's sake (and my wife's sake—she travels with me), I've committed to not repeatedly reusing a few favorite sermons. Fresh sermons help keep the preacher fresh.

Most preachers admit to being crazy busy at times. Few would suspect they could be busy and lazy at the same time. But if we fail to stay self-aware and self-disciplined, if we allow others to run our schedules or allow ourselves to squander study time, we can actually become lazy preachers—even when we are busy pastors.

6
STAGNATING

Some baseball players never seem to live up to their potential. In spite of having God-given talents to excel, they never do. They may be drafted by a major league team, show flashes of greatness, even have a respectable, journeyman career. But they fail to reach their full potential. They stagnate and remain underachievers.

That could have been José Bautista's story if it weren't for Dwayne Murphy. In a 2015 ESPN piece entitled "How Jose Bautista became Jose Bautista," Dave Schoenfield chronicles Bautista's early years as a pro.[1] After bouncing around the minors for several

1. David Schoenfield, "How Jose Bautista became Jose Bautista," *Espn.com*, October 19, 2015, http://espn.go.com/blog/sweetspot/post/_/id/64975/how-jose-bautista-became-jose-bautista.

years, he made the roster of the Pittsburgh Pirates in 2006. For several seasons he played a backup role, hitting just over a dozen home runs each year. When he was picked up by the Toronto Blue Jays in 2008, no one saw him as a rising superstar. A good utility player, for sure. But a starter—highly unlikely!

All that changed when the Jays' batting coach, Dwayne Murphy, started working with José. Murphy watched Bautista closely and noticed he generated great torque with his hip rotation but was slow in bringing his hands around. Murphy had Bautista relax and start his swing earlier by moving his top hand in a small semicircle about a second earlier than he had been doing. This small change would make a big difference.

Granted, it took weeks for José to get comfortable with this new swing. But when he did, the results were stunning. He hit twelve home runs in one month and developed into one of the best hitters in baseball for most of his career.

When it comes to realizing potential, preachers share something in common with major league ballplayers. We may be drafted by a local church, show flashes of homiletical excellence, and even become respected, journeyman pastors. But we can fail to reach our full potential as preachers; we can be homiletical underachievers.

That's why, like elite athletes, we can benefit from a coach. That's why we need a Dwayne Murphy.

WHO IS YOUR DWAYNE?

In my role at Heritage College and Seminary, I listen to many preachers—both at the school and in churches. I've never heard a preacher yet (including yours truly) who wouldn't benefit from coaching. Many preachers have strong, God-given gifts; however, all of us have specific habits and systemic patterns that keep us from hitting our potential. Like José Bautista before Dwayne Murphy, we swing hard but don't connect as often as we'd like. In short, we would benefit from some coaching.

A preaching coach doesn't have to be a better preacher than you are. When he was a player, Dwayne Murphy only hit half as many home runs as José Bautista. Yet good preaching coaches have two qualities that make them so useful. First, they know what a home-run sermon looks like. They understand the mechanics of sermon construction and sermon delivery. Second, they can spot exactly where a preacher is a bit off in his sermonic swing. They can identify, in specific terms, strong points and weak spots in a sermon. As a result, they can give customized counsel that goes far beyond the "Good sermon, Pastor" we sometimes hear at the door.

So let me ask you, preacher to preacher: Who gives you wise, knowledgeable feedback on your sermons? Who roots for your success as a preacher by helping you root out the bad habits in your preaching? Who is your Dwayne Murphy?

It's great to read books and blogs on preaching. It's wise to watch sermons from those who excel at biblical exposition. But nothing will bring more help than personalized, wise input from a coach.

WHY WE DON'T HAVE A DWAYNE

Many preachers would agree a coach could help, but will never get any coaching. Why not? There are likely many reasons, but let me focus on two.

First, we don't know whom to ask. Where do we find the preaching equivalent of a batting coach? Should we ask a pastoral peer who may not be any better at preaching than we are? A homiletics prof at a local seminary? How about an all-star preacher we've heard preach but don't know personally? While finding the right coach can be a challenge, it's not our major hindrance. I'm convinced there's a deeper reason, one that gets to another test of our hearts.

Second, we don't really want feedback. We feel uneasy about having someone scrutinize our sermons. Deep down, we live with insecurity about our preaching abilities. We know we aren't hitting home runs most Sundays, but at least we usually get good wood on the ball. So why should we invite criticism? Who finds joy in finding out the flaws in their sermonic swing? On top of that, most people in the congregation seem generally content with our level of preaching. They may not be cheering, but they aren't booing either—at least not loud enough for us to hear. So we play it safe and choose not to seek out an informed analysis of our preaching.

Here's what I've discovered about these two objections. Once we deal with our self-protective reluctance to receive coaching, we discover it's easier to find a coach than we expected. Once we've opened ourselves up to be coached, we've passed a test of the heart by confronting the temptation to stagnate and underachieve as preachers.

FINDING A DWAYNE

How do you go about engaging a preaching coach? Let me answer by telling you about an assignment I give to couples during their premarital counseling. I tell the engaged couple to identify a married couple whose marriage seems strong and satisfying. Then they are to approach this seasoned married couple with a request: "We want to develop a solid marriage, and we admire what we see in you. Could we take you out for coffee one time and talk about building a strong marriage?"

In my years of premarital counseling, I've never known an engaged couple to be turned down, even when they don't personally know the older couple. In fact, the seasoned couple is generally delighted to be asked. They've worked hard on their marriage and are eager to see others flourish. While they initially might only agree to meet once, the relationship between the couples often turns out to be long-lasting. The young couple now has a marriage coach!

My advice to preachers looking for a preaching coach is similar: prayerfully identify a preacher in your circle of relationships (geographical, denominational) whose preaching ministry you admire. Approach him with a request: "I want to grow as a preacher, and I appreciate what I hear in your sermons. Could I take you out for coffee one time and talk to you about becoming a more effective preacher?"

Most preachers you ask will be encouraged by your affirmation and willing to have a conversation about effective preaching. Come to the conversation with a list of questions: How do you approach your preparation? How do you move from exegesis to exposition, from studying a text to structuring a sermon? How has God shaped your soul as a preacher? What do you know now that you wished you had known earlier?

Over the course of the conversation you will sense if this preacher could be a helpful coach. Is there good chemistry? Honesty? Candor? If so, ask him to watch or listen to one of your sermons and give you some feedback. Invite him to point out what he sees as strengths of the sermon and ways it could be strengthened. Make sure to thank him for investing time and energy into your life and ministry.

So far, I've written about coaching as if you can have only one preaching coach. While one coach is one more than most preachers have, it's wise to think about assembling a coaching team. I've read that PGA golfer Phil Mickelson has a team of coaches who help him with various aspects of his game. Over the course of my ministry, I've received coaching from professors, peers, and my wife.[2] Each has provided a blend of encouragement and challenge, helping me to improve as a preacher.

When Paul wrote a letter to give Timothy some personalized coaching, he told him to work hard at preaching and teaching. He challenged Timothy not to stagnate or underachieve as a

2. See chapter 21, "Listen to Your Closest Ally."

preacher. The outcome, Paul said, was that people in the congregation would see his progress (1 Timothy 4:15). They would be able to say, "He's a better preacher this year than he was last year." If you continue to grow as a preacher, getting some coaching along the way, the people in your congregation will be able to say the same thing about you.

7

SPEAKING ONE LANGUAGE

To be truly effective as a preacher, I'm convinced you must become bilingual—fluent in two languages. While you may only use one language throughout the week, you'll need two on Sundays. I say that even though when it comes to languages, I only speak English.

What are the two languages a preacher must speak? Not English and French (even in Canada). Not Greek and Hebrew (though learning to *read* both is a great help to any preacher). The two languages a preacher must speak fluently are grace and truth. I say that because Jesus was fluent in both. Scripture tells us he "was full of grace and truth" (John 1:14). But while Jesus was equally fluent in the vocabulary of grace *and* truth, most of us are not. We typically have either grace *or* truth as our mother tongue. We may speak one without an accent; however, the other is somewhat foreign to us. As a result, we fail to communicate the fullness of God's Word. Thankfully, learning to preach in both grace and truth is doable, even for those of us who only speak English. Adding a second language will challenge us in deep ways. Speaking both grace *and* truth qualifies as one of the tests of a preacher's heart.

IDENTIFYING OUR MOTHER TONGUE

The first step toward becoming bilingual as a preacher is identifying your "mother tongue." Often in homiletics courses, I draw a long, straight line on the whiteboard. At one end, I write the word "prophetic." Preachers whose first language is truth excel in emphasizing God's revealed will. In every sermon, they highlight God's righteous standards and expose our failure to reach it. Like biblical prophets, they call people to turn from sin and turn back to God.

At the other end of the continuum, I write "pastoral." Preachers whose native language is grace convey warm-hearted compassion through their words, tone, and gestures. No matter the passage, their words come accented with grace. In a pastoral way, they speak hope into broken hearts.

Both languages have their own unique dangers. Preachers strong in trumpeting truth can leave listeners feeling chastened and defeated. People in their congregations may try to muscle up spiritually in their own strength and be tempted to give up when their strength fails. On the other hand, preachers who gravitate toward grace tend to underemphasize God's holy demands. Over time, their congregations can become complacent and self-satisfied.

In the classroom, I explain that all preachers fall somewhere on the continuum between prophetic ("truth-telling") and pastoral ("grace-giving"). I ask each student to take a marker and write their initials somewhere along the line, indicating where they fall on the continuum. I tell them they can't put their initials exactly in the middle of the line; only Jesus had the perfect balance of both.

No matter where they place themselves, I urge students not to settle for preaching only in their default dialect—whether pastoral or prophetic. Unless preachers communicate both grace and truth, they will not faithfully represent Scripture.

ADOPTING THE LANGUAGE OF THE TEXT

Just as the Living Word was full of grace and truth, so is the written Word. That's why Jeremiah compared God's Word to both grain and a hammer; it nourishes and shatters (Jeremiah 23:28–29). That's why Paul could tell Timothy, "All Scripture is breathed out by God and profitable for teaching, for reproof, for correction, and for training in righteousness" (2 Timothy 3:16). Since Scripture communicates both God's grace and his truth, preachers must as well.

If Scripture communicates both grace and truth, how does a preacher choose which language to emphasize in a sermon?

The preacher doesn't get to choose; the passage does.[1] A preacher's job is to accurately convey what God communicates in a section of Scripture. This means we must not only get the message of the passage right in our sermons, we must get the mood right as well.

If we preach Psalm 23 in a way that leaves people feeling shaken up and convicted, we've not been true to the tone of the text. Conversely, if we fail to preach the opening verses in James 4 ("You adulterous people!") in a way that convicts and corrects, we've misrepresented the text. Preachers must become bilingual if they hope to faithfully proclaim "the whole counsel of God" (Acts 20:27).

I mentioned at the outset that I only speak one language. For years, I was monolingual as a preacher as well. I only spoke the language of grace. Both by temperament and theology, I gravitated to grace. I wanted to bring people hope and healing, so I highlighted the grace of God. People responded positively. The church grew. What could be wrong with that?

But every once in a while, my wife would comment how last week's sermon didn't accurately reflect the passage I had preached. The text had come down hard on sin, but my sermon had not. She wondered why I hadn't reflected the strong words in the Scripture. Why had I let people off so easily? I usually responded defensively, protesting that I tried to bring out the challenge given in the passage. Occasionally, someone in

---

1. For guidance on how to choose a passage, see chapter 17, "Devote Yourself to Prayer and the Word."

the congregation would say the same thing my wife had been trying to tell me. To my chagrin, I had to admit she had been right. I tended to magnify grace and mute truth. I was often pastoral, rarely prophetic. I needed to become bilingual.

LEARNING A SECOND LANGUAGE

How does a preacher who is strong in one of the two essential languages learn to preach well in the other? While I'm still learning to speak fluently and forcefully with a prophetic edge, here are some of the things I've found helpful.

First, commit yourself to taking your tone from the passage itself. Look for words indicating the author's emotional emphasis and then follow his lead. If the passage has a pastoral feel, let that come out in your sermon. If it shakes people up with prophetic fervor, let your sermon do the same. To faithfully exposit a text, you need to convey both the message and the mood of the text.

Second, listen to preachers who excel in the language you are trying to learn. I have found several expositors who bring a strong prophetic edge to their sermons without giving up on grace. While I can't clone them, I've tried to learn from them.

Third, remember that learning a second language takes practice and causes discomfort. You will feel conspicuous and awkward at times. You will be tempted to revert to what comes most naturally to you. But push on to become homiletically bilingual. Prayerfully rely on Christ to help you be Christ-like in preaching with both grace and truth. Like all who learn a second language, you'll be glad you did.

Finally, remember that even as you add a second language, you'll never lose your first one. I still smile when I think of a preaching experience in Kenya. I spoke in a church where the host preacher thundered as he addressed the congregation. Right before I stood to speak, my wife leaned over and encouraged me to "bring it" as I preached. As the saying goes, "when in Rome. ..." So, I preached with all the prophetic fervor I could muster. I tried to thunder. When I finished, the pastor of the church came up to close the service. He said, "The Bible tells us God sometimes speaks in fire, earthquake, or a strong wind. And sometimes God speaks in a gentle whisper. Today we have heard him speak in that gentle whisper." Even when I thought I was trying to be more prophetic, my pastoral mother tongue still came through.

PREACHING IN TWO LANGUAGES AT ONCE

G. K. Chesterton was fond of pointing out how the Christian faith paradoxically brings together seeming opposites. As he put it, Christianity has a unique way of "combining furious opposites, by keeping them both, and keeping them both furious."[2] This is what a preacher must do with grace and truth.

Our goal is to become so fluent in both grace and truth that we can speak both in the same sermon. We seamlessly shift between the two, giving grace and telling truth when prompted by our text. We preach with both pastoral earnestness and a prophetic edge. We don't blend grace and truth in a way that

---

2. G. K. Chesterton, *Orthodoxy* (Glasgow: William Collins Sons & Co., 1961), 93.

dilutes them. Rather, we combine them in a way that keeps them both furiously full-strength.

There's a Greek word that captures what we are seeking to do: *parakaleō*. It's difficult to capture the range of the term in a single English word. Sometimes it can have the nuance of exhortation (Acts 2:40). At other times it emphasizes encouragement (Acts 16:40). *Parakaleō* preaching brings grace and truth together by giving people both encouragement and exhortation. It has a prophetic edge, but the edge is not serrated. While it can cut to the heart, the incisions are surgical and healing. At the same time, *parakaleō* preaching is pastoral without being permissive. It normalizes our struggles without normalizing our sin.

When it comes to languages, I still have to admit I'm monolingual: only English. But when it comes to preaching, I'm becoming bilingual. You can too! That's a wonderful truth, and it's all by God's grace.

8
FEAR

"Deer in the headlights" is a rather accurate description of how most of us felt during our first attempts at preaching. We looked out at the congregation and saw all eyes fixed on us, like so many sets of oncoming headlights. We stood behind the pulpit or podium, immobilized by fear. Some of us were literally scared stiff.

I know all about this "deer-in-the-headlights" fear. When I first began preaching, my throat would tighten, the pitch of my voice would rise, and I would swallow involuntarily in the middle of sentences. I stayed tethered to the pulpit and tied to my notes. I wanted to gain greater freedom in my delivery, but didn't know how.

Facing down our fears to gain greater freedom in preaching is not just a challenge for rookies. Even veteran preachers struggle. Sure, we get more comfortable than we were at first. But we still find ourselves taking cover behind a pulpit, podium, or music stand. We still repeatedly look down at our notes. Our delivery remains reserved and inhibited; we never really cut loose. We're not exactly a deer in the headlights, but neither are we "hind's feet on high places."

Overcoming the fear that keeps us muted in our delivery and manacled to our manuscripts is one of the heart tests a preacher will face.

IS FREEDOM POSSIBLE?

Most preachers would like to be free from their notes and free in their delivery. But they don't see this kind of freedom as a realistic option. The reasons given for staying tied down and tethered to sermon notes seem valid, even noble. See if you hear your own internal objections as you read these three excuses.

1. "I want to get it right. After all, I am preaching the Word of God. I've worked hard to understand the passage and craft a sermon that cogently and clearly presents the truth of the passage. I've manuscripted my message, even wordsmithing some lines to make them as vivid and memorable as possible. If I go without notes, I'll likely leave out important parts or won't say them as well as I've written them down. I want my hearers to get the

best of my homiletical labors. If I don't stay close to my notes, I'll be giving people less than my best."

2. "I don't have a good memory. I've never excelled in memorizing anything—not Bible verses in Awana or class notes in seminary. Hats off to those who have been blessed with a photographic memory, but I'm not in that elite group. Others may be able to preach well without notes, but not me. Sure, I'd love to do so, but I just don't have the ability."

3. "I don't want to embarrass myself. I've watched preachers lose their way in the middle of a message. I've felt the awkward silence, seen the panicked look on the preacher's face. I sometimes have nightmares where I'm preaching a sermon, can't find my notes, and don't remember what I'm supposed to say next. I don't want to be a pulpit version of Peter trying to walk on the homiletical waters only to sink in a very public way. Better to stay in the boat, where the safety of my sermon notes help to keep me afloat."

IS FREEDOM FROM NOTES ALL THAT IMPORTANT ANYWAY?

Given these understandable objections, why should we torment ourselves (and our hearers) with attempts to preach free from our sermon notes? Here's the answer: to free up our delivery and increase the impact of our sermons.

Gareth Malone is a choral music specialist in the UK. In his *Guide to Classical Music*, he makes an interesting observation about instrumental soloists: they usually play without a score. The rest of the orchestra may have music stands and musical scores in front of them, but not the soloists. They stand on stage with nothing between them and the audience.

Why do these soloists forgo a copy of the music, especially when they have such an extensive amount of playing time? Malone explains the decision to play without a musical manuscript as "mainly a form of sustained communication with the audience." He notes that if a soloist stays "hidden behind a music stand with their head buried in the score it can make it harder to reach the audience."[1]

Reaching the audience pushes soloists to play without a score. Reaching the audience should also push preachers to get free from their notes. Looking people in the eye helps you connect with their hearts. Just try having a conversation with someone while looking down as you speak. How does it go?

The desire to connect more deeply with our hearers should move us to get free from our sermon notes. Our motivation is not to impress but to impact. We don't seek to draw attention to ourselves but to better serve our listeners. Ironically, when tied to our notes, we actually draw more attention to ourselves!

---

1. Gareth Malone, *Gareth Malone's Guide to Classical Music* (London: HarperCollins, 2013), Kindle loc. 191.

A DOABLE CHALLENGE

Up to this point, you may be feeling I'm adding more pressure to your life as a preacher. Preaching free from our notes seems as farfetched to many of us as running a four-minute mile or hitting a hole in one. It's already hard enough to prepare a quality sermon. Now we are expected to memorize it? Why raise the bar to a height we can't possibly clear?

Let me highlight two things that may change your perspective. First, getting free from your notes is more about internalization than memorization. Second, getting free from your notes can be done incrementally.

Internalizing rather than memorizing. As a young associate pastor fresh out of seminary, I was given occasional opportunities to preach on Sunday mornings. Because I had several weeks to get ready, I sought to memorize my manuscript and preach without notes.

On the Sunday I was scheduled to preach, I tried to avoid conversations with people in the congregation before the service. I made my way through the sanctuary like a waiter carrying a platter full of meals in a crowded restaurant, afraid someone might jostle me, upsetting the fragile balancing act I had going on in my brain. When I preached the message, I worked hard to say everything just like I had written and memorized it. Almost word perfect.

There was only one problem. My wife commented that, as I delivered the sermon, it felt like I read my manuscript off the back of my eyelids, like I had an invisible teleprompter inside my head. Rather than connecting with my hearers, I was concentrating hard on my memorized message. My delivery may have been note free, but it felt mechanical.

So I made a shift. Rather than memorize the sermon, I decided to internalize it. I still manuscripted my message, as writing is an exercise in clear thinking. However, I no longer aimed at word-for-word memorization. I went for internalization.

Internalizing a message involves getting clear on the overall flow of thought in your sermon. Think of internalizing the floor plan of your house. You can think your way through a tour of the various rooms of your home, right? The entryway leads to the kitchen. Off the kitchen is the living room. Down the hall are three bedrooms and a bathroom.

Internalizing a sermon begins by getting clear on the floor plan of your message. For example:

- After your introduction, read the text.
- Next you state your first point.
- Then you show how this idea comes from the first two verses of the text, explaining a key term that needs clarification.
- Then you tell the story of last summer's road trip to Atlanta to illustrate the concept of pressing on when you get weary and tired.
- After that comes a transition to the second point (and so on).

When you can walk yourself through the layout of the message, you are well on your way to internalizing it. By the way, I've found by the time I've manuscripted a sermon, I've internalized a good portion of it. The process of carefully writing out my thoughts embeds much of the message into my mind.

Internalizing means knowing your message *thought for thought* rather than *word for word*. While there will be some sentences you want to say with precision (your main points, or a turn of phrase), your goal is to *paraphrase* your manuscript. This allows you to stay free from your notes but still stay true to them. Your delivery seems more like a conversation and less like a canned presentation.

Prioritizing what you internalize. Here's a second piece of good news that makes getting free from sermon notes less daunting: you can do this incrementally rather than all at once. Instead of trying to go from note-dependent to note-free in one giant leap, take it in smaller steps. Prioritize what you internalize.

As I've already said, begin by internalizing the overall structure (floor plan) of the message. Once you can think your way through the flow of the message, you will already feel less tied to your notes. You will no longer fear getting lost in the middle of your message since you know (in general terms) what comes next!

After you have internalized the overall structure of the sermon, I'd encourage you to internalize your introduction and conclusion.

This allows you to connect eye-to-eye and heart-to-heart with your listeners at key moments of the message. As John Broadus observed in his classic book on homiletics, "People like for the minister to look at them and to share directly with them. It is difficult to overestimate the importance of eye contact."[2]

When you get comfortable being free from your notes at the start and conclusion of the sermon, take the next step. Internalize your main points. Or internalize your illustrations.

Without putting too much pressure on yourself, push yourself to increase the amount you internalize. In time, you'll discover you have become much less dependent on your sermon notes but are still communicating the essential message you've prepared.

A SAFETY NET

Being free from your sermon notes is not the same as preaching with no notes. I've found it helpful to transfer the outline (floor plan) of my message to an oversized Post-It note. I stick this note inside my Bible, on the page of the text I'm preaching. This gives me a safety net in case I go into memory free fall at some point in the message. On a good week, I won't need to glance at it. On other weeks, I'm glad it's there.

I get the fact that we all have different capabilities when it comes to memory work. I also am learning that age makes the

---

2. John Broadus, *On the Preparation and Delivery of Sermons*, 4th ed. (London: HarperOne, 1979), 270.

process more challenging. But I remain convinced that most preachers could become far less note-dependent than they imagine possible. Someone once said memory is like a trusted friend. The more you rely on it, the more reliable it proves.

So in order to free yourself up in your delivery and increase your connection with your hearers, make it your goal to become increasingly free from your notes. And when you start to fear you can't possibly do this, remember what Paul wrote to a gifted but fearful preacher named Timothy: "For this reason I remind you to fan into flame the gift of God, which is in you through the laying on of my hands, for God gave us a spirit not of fear but of power and love and self-control" (2 Timothy 1:6–7).

9
RETREATING

I remember a conversation with a group of recent seminary grads, all of whom were promising young preachers but still felt like subpar leaders. They expressed a great deal of self-doubt and defeat as they spoke of trying to lead their congregations forward. They excelled when it came to solving exegetical problems; they struggled when it came to resolving congregational ones. They saw the need for solid pastoral leadership but lacked the confidence they could meet the need.

Over the years, I've discovered this kind of leadership uncertainty is widespread among preachers. Many of us feel inadequate when it comes to providing visionary, directional leadership for the churches we serve. As a result, we often retreat from the messy, difficult work of pastoral leadership.

We choose to focus on the caring and feeding aspects of pastoral ministry, leaving the leadership side of shepherding to others—either to those on the church board or to a self-appointed "church boss."

Early in my pastoral ministry, I felt the temptation to retreat from leading. The church I pastored was going through growing pains that called for stronger leadership than I thought I could provide. I was quite intimidated by several older men in the congregation who were resisting the changes I was championing. Differing viewpoints were causing relational tension. I was frightened and shaken by it all.

Providentially, my homiletics professor from seminary happened to be traveling through our area. Over breakfast at a local restaurant, I poured out my fears and frustrations about the challenges I was facing. He listened carefully and then challenged me to grow as a pastoral leader. His words, as I remember them, went like this: "Rick, God has given you a high capacity for bearing fruit as a preacher. But your fruitfulness as a preacher will be limited if you don't develop and deepen your roots as a leader."

That conversation had a life-changing impact. It convinced me leadership was an essential part of my role as a shepherd. While it didn't diminish my passion for preaching, it enlarged my desire to become a better pastoral leader. I determined to stop retreating and start growing as a leader. I began a journey that continues to this day.

One of the happy realizations I've made about pastoral leadership is that preaching God's Word is a vital part of leading

God's people. While preaching and leading are different functions, they do overlap. In fact, the two merge and augment one
another in surprising ways. This means pastors can lead from
the pulpit. And we can do this without diminishing our commitment to faithful exposition of God's Word.

How can biblical preaching help us resist the temptation to
retreat from our role in congregational leadership? Here are
four primary ways.

VISION SETTING

Preaching sets the vision for the congregation, but not in the
way some think. Expository preaching doesn't turn sermon
time into vision talks. It doesn't expound strategic plans in
place of Scripture. When it comes to setting vision, expositors do something far less overt, but far more important. They
preach God's vision and mission for his people.

When I first stepped into the role of a lead pastor, the popular
books on pastoring emphasized the importance of developing
a compelling vision statement for a local congregation. I remember talking with a more seasoned pastor about how I should go
about setting the congregational vision. He cautioned me with
some sage advice. He warned me that the people in my new
congregation would likely be wary if I, as a young pastor, came
in talking of some new, grand vision for the church. They had
seen this before. So he counseled me not to rush into crafting a
new vision or mission statement. Instead, he encouraged me to
preach the Word in a way that gave people God's vision for the
church and for his mission in the world.

I took his advice. I began my ministry in this new church preaching through passages in the book of Luke, focusing on Jesus' vision for life and ministry. Each Sunday, the message highlighted some aspect of Jesus' view of people and his mission to seek and save the lost. Slowly, our church family began to develop a ministry vision inspired by Jesus' priorities and purpose, and we were able to articulate this understanding into a more formal vision and mission statement. We based our statement on our shared understanding of God's will for his church as seen in Scripture. Preaching had led the way.

CLIMATE CHANGE

Every congregation has an internal climate. But not every church's climate is as warm and welcoming as it should be. Some are frosty, with a perpetual wintry feel. People stay bundled up and hidden from one another. In other churches, the relational warmth is only for those who have been there long enough to become acclimated. Newcomers are left out in the cold.

Pastors have the opportunity to bring about climate change through their preaching. Each week, as they communicate God's Word and God's heart, they help set the spiritual temperature of the worship service. Biblical preaching brings a congregation into the light of God's truth and the warmth of his grace.

Several years ago, a friend of mine became the pastor of a church that had experienced a considerable amount of turmoil and trauma. The congregation had become fragmented, somewhat distant and detached. Visitors left feeling unnoticed and unable to connect. Thankfully, my friend was one of the most caring shepherds I've ever known. Each week, he faithfully preached God's Word. As he did, he not only communicated God's truth but did it in a relationally engaging way. In time, he began to rub off on others. His warmth warmed up the rest of the congregation. The climate began to change for the better.

Jesus made it clear that a disciple, once fully trained, will be like his teacher (Luke 6:40). We reproduce after our own kind. That means, over time, churches begin to take on the personality and passion of the pastor. Preachers set the climate for the congregation—that's called leadership.

GOSPEL FOCUS

How does a congregation grow in its passion for reaching lost people with the life-saving message of Christ? Gospel preaching is part of the answer. And this kind of gospel preaching can be done by pastors committed to exposition. The key is learning to make a "gospel move" as part of an expository sermon.

By "gospel move," I mean that, at some point in the message, the preacher points people to Christ and his redemptive work. It's not that the preacher ignores the immediate context or original message of the passage. Instead, the preacher points to Christ and his gospel as a part of the exposition of the passage.

The theological rationale for this emphasis comes from the conviction that the larger metanarrative of the Bible is the story of the gospel. As Jesus declared, every part of Scripture points to him

(John 5:39). That means there is a pathway that leads to Christ in every passage of Scripture. Or to change the picture, the gospel grows organically out of the soil of every text we preach.

As preachers regularly highlight the gospel in their sermons, they lead their congregations to become more gospel focused. They avoid what Don Carson calls the trap of "assuming the gospel"—which can eventually lead a congregation to abandon the gospel. Preachers who regularly rehearse the good news of the gospel provide people with a solid footing for their faith.

But there's also a leadership benefit that comes to a church when a pastor regularly makes a gospel move in his messages. People in the congregation gain more confidence to invite friends to church who have not yet come to know Christ in a saving way. This confidence comes from knowing that the pastor will present the good news of the gospel as part of the morning expository message on any given Sunday. Gospel presentations are not confined to Easter or Christmas. In a sense, every service becomes an outreach service, even though the focus of the message is expositing a passage for believers.

As preachers regularly and repeatedly bring out the good news of the gospel in their sermons, they lead the congregation to be more gospel focused. Once again, preaching overlaps with leading.

CALL TO ACTION

Faithful preaching is not content with only informing the mind; it seeks to transform the life. Life change is always a primary goal of biblical exposition. This means preachers who explain and apply Scripture serve as teachers and leaders at the same time.

Calling people to obedient action in response to God's Word will test our hearts as preachers. Will we graciously, but courageously, proclaim the truth—even when it confronts and convicts? Or will we tone down the text, blunting the force of biblical commands?

I remember the day a pastoral colleague called me out for turning God's commands into suggestions. Between our two morning services, he told me, "Rick, you say 'I'd suggest' too often." When I asked him to explain, he replied, "You often finish your sermon by asking, 'So how should we respond to what God is saying to us in this passage? Well, I'd suggest ...'" Then he added, "When God commands, it's not a suggestion."

To be faithful preachers and effective leaders, we must present God's truth in its stark beauty, not bleaching the bold colors out of biblical commands and turning them into pastel suggestions. We will need to challenge our hearers to become "doers of the word and not hearers only" (James 1:22). We will call individuals and the entire church family to act in obedient faith. In this way, we will not only serve as faithful expositors of God's Word, but will also provide pastoral leadership for God's people.

LEADING RATHER THAN RETREATING

It is true that good preachers are not automatically good leaders. Leadership involves developing abilities and skills which are not identical to those required for preaching.

But even those of us who aren't exceptionally gifted as leaders can still fulfill the leadership side of our calling as shepherds. We do that, in part, through our faithful preaching of God's Word. Rather than retreating from the challenges and demands of congregational leadership, we can choose to grow as leaders and learn to lead through our preaching.

10
CRITICISM

Preachers can count on being critiqued. In some ways, it's only fair. Preaching, by its very nature, takes place in a public forum. And going public with our thoughts—even when seeking to exposit God's Word—opens us to public response. Since we can't expect only positive feedback, we must anticipate some level of criticism. This brings us to another test of a preacher's heart: How will we respond to the criticism we receive as preachers?

While painful, criticism can actually bring great profit to preachers. The bruising can produce blessing—if we respond well. And the starting place for a healthy response to criticism involves developing a biblical view of correction.

A BIBLICAL VIEW OF CORRECTION

Correction emerges as a major theme in the book of Proverbs. "Whoever loves discipline loves knowledge, but he who hates reproof is stupid" (12:1). "The ear that listens to life-giving reproof will dwell among the wise" (15:31). "Do you see a man who is wise in his own eyes? There is more hope for a fool than for him" (26:12). That's just a sampling, but it highlights an important truth: correction is essential for wisdom and growth. Conversely, those who reject rebuke head toward folly.

So while correction is rarely enjoyable, it still must be embraced. That's why we train preachers to profit from constructive correction in our homiletics courses at Heritage College and Seminary. After each sermon, we go through the same drill. We ask those who just heard the message to answer two questions: What did the preacher do well in this sermon? Where would you encourage further growth? Over the years, I've been impressed by the way students give and receive honest feedback. I'm hopeful this exercise will prepare them for the range of feedback they will hear when preaching to their congregations.

Let's get specific here, because talking about correction in a general way is too vague to be useful. The assessments and evaluations we receive as preachers come in several categories. Three of the most common are (1) content, (2) communication, and (3) character.

Content. When someone criticizes our content, they react to *what* we said. The apostle Paul received this kind of criticism. In Romans 3:8 he writes about being maligned for the content of his message: "And why not do evil that good may come?—as some people slanderously charge us with saying. Their condemnation is just." Paul's critics falsely accused him of preaching a twisted message of grace. Whether intentionally or not, they misunderstood his message and responded with unfounded criticism. Paul wrote it off ("Their condemnation is just") and went on preaching.

Sometimes, however, the critique of our content is justified. Just ask Apollos. Although Apollos qualified as a committed and capable preacher, his message was theologically deficient. He only knew about the baptism done by John (repentance baptism) and not the baptism commanded by Christ (Christian baptism). Thankfully, Priscilla and Aquila, a seasoned ministry couple, "took him aside and explained to him the way of God more accurately" (Acts 18:26). Their correction sought to equip rather than embarrass this promising young preacher. Evidently, Apollos humbly received it. Luke tells us that after being set straight by Aquila and Priscilla, Apollos went on to preach with great effectiveness in Corinth (Acts 18:27–28).

When our sermon content gets criticized, we should consider whether we were actually mistaken or simply misunderstood. In either case, content criticism challenges us to strive for biblical accuracy and clarity in our sermons.

Communication. When someone critiques our communication, they assess *how* we spoke. The focus shifts from what we say to the way we speak. Paul faced this kind of critique as well: "For they say, 'His letters are weighty and strong, but his bodily presence is weak, and his speech of no account.'" (2 Corinthians 10:10).

This kind of critique calls us to continual growth as effective communicators of God's truth. While we cannot cater to everyone's tastes when it comes to communication style, we should listen for patterns in this kind of feedback. When we hear the same critique repeated by different people, we must take it seriously and consider it carefully.

Character. When someone criticizes our character, the concern moves from *what* we said (content) or *how* we spoke (communication) to *who* we are. This type of criticism ranks as the most painful of all. Once again, Paul faced this kind of blistering rebuke. When on trial before the Roman governor, Felix, a lawyer named Tertullus lit into him, directly attacking his character: "For we have found this man a plague, one who stirs up riots among all the Jews throughout the world" (Acts 24:5).

Most preachers I know have never been accused of stirring up riots, but many of us have had our characters maligned. Paul's response to Tertullus shows that sometimes this kind of critique must be countered and refuted (Acts 24:10–21). However, the proverbs quoted above warn us against quickly writing off any who question our character. If we become wise in our own eyes, we play the fool and will suffer for it (Proverbs 26:12). All of us can benefit from the refining fire God allows to come our way in the form of criticism.

CONSIDERING THE SOURCE

Not all critiques are created equal. The old maxim about considering the source applies to critics and criticism. Just as it helps to evaluate the kind of criticism we receive (content, communication, or character), it's also wise to consider the source. Here are four common critics preachers can expect to meet along the way.

Anonymous critics shoot from the shadows. They place unsigned notes in the offering plate or send letters with no signature or return address.

Analysts don't see themselves as critical, just concerned about accuracy. They delight in pointing out areas where a preacher misspoke. They rush up right after the sermon to tell the preacher he gave the wrong month for the moon landing in his opening illustration. Analysts are picky about particulars and tactless in their timing.

Antagonists mean to be critical. For reasons we may or may not know, they've become hard and cynical toward us. They no longer give us the benefit of the doubt. They interpret our words in the worst possible way. If they listen closely to our sermons, it's only to look for ammunition to fire back at us. These folks can break our hearts and boil our blood—at the same time.

Allies remain on our side even when they get on our case. Their words can hurt but they never mean to be hurtful. Proverbs 27:6 speaks about allies when it says, "Faithful are the wounds of a friend; profuse are the kisses of an enemy." If married, your spouse should be your closest ally.[1]

---

1. See chapter 21, "Listen to Your Closest Ally."

RESPONDING TO CORRECTION

Since all preachers can expect criticism, all of us need to learn to respond in a godly, healthy way: staying gracious and humble, willing to listen to words of reproof. A soft answer does generally turn away wrath (Proverbs 15:1).

I find it helpful to remember that different types of critics call for different kinds of responses. Let me run through each of the four categories of critics and suggest constructive ways to respond to each one.

Anonymous. If someone is unwilling to own up to his or her critique, I don't feel obligated to give it much weight. In fact, a scathing, unsigned letter may best remain unread. Another option involves giving the letter to an ally to read. This allows someone you trust to filter the criticism and distill any valid comments.

Analysts. I've found analysts are normally harmless and genuinely want to help. What they say often has validity; however, their comments can also be relatively unimportant and poorly timed. If their input comes infrequently, pastoral wisdom calls us to graciously hear what they have to say, thank them, and move on. However, if they start making comments on a regular basis, set gracious but firm boundaries. The goal is not to punish them or turn them into antagonists, but to help them become more tactful in what they say and when they say it.

Antagonists. When dealing with antagonists, don't try to go it alone. Alert other leaders to the situation and ask for help. One of the reasons God designed the church to be led by a group of elders was to guard against "fierce wolves" (Acts 20:28–29). Elders and other wise allies can help determine how to best respond to antagonists—seeking resolution while providing protection.

Allies. When an ally speaks a word of correction, listen closely and respond gratefully. Wise pastors identify allies in the congregation and invite them to offer constructive feedback on their preaching and other aspects of their pastoral ministry.

As a young pastor, God blessed me with the gift of an older, godly man as one of my closest allies. When he spoke words of correction, they were always well-timed and well-intentioned. Usually, they were also on the mark. I remember telling him that, if he ever had a concern or critique, he had an open invitation to come to me directly. Like Aquila with Apollos, he occasionally took me aside and provided wise guidance. I became a better pastor and preacher because of his feedback.

As preachers, we can't avoid criticism. But instead of letting this test frustrate us, we can seek to understand it and profit from it. If we do, we will not only become better preachers and pastors, but better people as well.

11
DISENGAGED LISTENERS

Most people think of preaching as a monologue, though it is actually a dialogue. The preacher may be doing all the talking, but he's not doing all the communicating. As we all know, a great deal of communication is non-verbal. So even as the preacher speaks, the people in the congregation are having their say as well.

It's a joy to preach to people who communicate they are fully engaged with the message by their posture and facial expressions. They lean forward, nod their heads, smile, and—in some congregations—speak words of affirmation ("That's right!" "Amen!" "Preach it!").

On the other hand, it's discouraging to preach to people whose body language shouts their disengagement. Their heads stay down and eyes remain closed—but probably not in prayer. They repeatedly check their phones—but likely not to take notes. While still physically present, they've already checked out and gone home.

Preaching to the disengaged tests the heart of a preacher. How should we respond to those who seem unresponsive? How do we avoid being distracted by those who appear disengaged?

Two types of disengaged hearers especially jostle my soul, upsetting my internal equilibrium as I preach: the dozing and the disgruntled. Both will eventually show up at your church. Both are unsettling, but in different ways. So to pass this heart test as a preacher, we will need to learn how to respond to both the dozing and the disgruntled.

PREACHING TO THE DOZING

A number of years ago, a group of men from our church spent a week in Mexico doing construction on a church building. After working all day, we made our beds in sleeping bags on the sanctuary's concrete floor. Each morning, guys woke up stiff and sore, complaining they didn't get much sleep the night before. I recall smiling and saying, "It surprises me you all had such trouble sleeping last night; back home, some of you sleep very well in our sanctuary on Sunday mornings."

It's hard not to be distracted by people who drift off to dreamland during our sermons. It's disconcerting to preach to a woman fast asleep—head back, mouth wide open. Or a man fighting to stay awake, his head repeatedly jerking up after nodding off. You almost want to break from your prepared message and loudly quote Ephesians 5:14: "Awake, O sleeper, and arise from the dead, and Christ will shine on you." However, that would be both exegetically unsound and pastorally unwise!

How should we deal with the dozing as we preach? By preaching with compassion and passion.

Preach with compassion. I find it helpful to remember I don't know the backstory or life challenges faced by most of the people who show up on Sundays. However, I can count on the fact that some show up running on fumes. Hectic schedules, crazy work shifts, sick kids, and lingering illnesses lead some to arrive physically and emotionally exhausted. They have made a heroic effort just to come at all. When they finally sit down and slow up, fatigue overwhelms and sleep comes easy.

The Gospels record how Peter, James, and John kept nodding off while Jesus poured out his heart in prayer in the garden of Gethsemane. While they must have been embarrassed when Jesus rebuked them, they still couldn't keep their eyes open. "And again he came and found them sleeping, for their eyes were heavy" (Matthew 26:43). I imagine most of us have found ourselves dozing off when we should be fervently praying or attentively listening. As Jesus explains: "The spirit indeed is willing, but the flesh is weak" (26:41).

So compassion is a better response than condemnation when we spot someone sleeping while we are preaching.

A compassionate heart that "remembers that we are dust" (Psalm 103:14) can relieve some of the inner turmoil we experience when preaching to the dozing.

Preach with passion. It's one thing to have a few dozers in the crowd; it's another problem if this becomes the norm rather than the exception. A sleepy congregation could indicate the real problem is not in the pew but in the pulpit.

Back in my seminary days, Professor Howard Hendricks used to tell us: "It's a sin to bore people with the Word of God."[1] Allowing for the Hendricks hyperbole, he still makes a good point. As preachers, we are charged with communicating the most important message of all. If we put people to sleep through our lack of clarity and passion, we are not faithfully conveying God's message. Disengaged, sleeping hearers should spur us to become more engaging preachers. People have a much more difficult time dozing off when the preacher passionately presents the message.

PREACHING TO THE DISGRUNTLED

Dozing listeners can be distracting—like having a fly buzzing around your head as you speak. Disgruntled listeners, however, are unsettling. They seem more like angry wasps than annoying flies.

---

1. Pedagogy class lecture by Dr. Howard Hendricks, Dallas Theological Seminary, 1984. This is a slight variation on a quote attributed to Hendricks's friend Jim Rayburn, the founder of Young Life: "It's a sin to bore a kid with the gospel."

At one church I pastored, a woman consistently crossed her arms as I spoke. Her expression was fixed in a permanent grimace. She never looked up, avoiding all eye contact with me. I knew she was unhappy with me and the direction the elders had set for the congregation. Each Sunday morning, her nonverbal communication shouted her displeasure. My experience is not unique. Pastor Andy Davis, in his book *Revitalize*, tells of a man with an explosive temper who promised to "fight [him] every step of the way" and "used to sit with his arms crossed and glare" as Andy preached.[2]

How do you preach with joy when you know someone is furious with you? How do you stay focused on your message when your mind gets distracted by a disgruntled person sitting unhappily in front of you?

Paul's words to Timothy prepare preachers for this exact scenario. "And the Lord's servant must not be quarrelsome but kind to everyone, able to teach, patiently enduring evil, correcting his opponents with gentleness. God may perhaps grant them repentance leading to a knowledge of the truth" (2 Timothy 2:24–25). In these verses, Paul reminds Timothy—and all preachers—of four important theological truths that steady us when speaking to those who oppose us.

Remember you represent Christ. A preacher is "the Lord's servant." We serve Christ—who warned us to expect some opposition: "A servant is not greater than his master. If they

---

2. Andy Davis, *Revitalize: Biblical Keys to Helping Your Church Come Alive Again* (Grand Rapids: Baker Books, 2017), 130.

persecuted me, they will also persecute you" (John 15:20). When Christ was reviled, "he did not revile in return" (1 Peter 2:23). Since we are his servants, our reactions to those who oppose us should emulate his.

Show kindness even when it's not reciprocated. I can't help but notice that 2 Timothy 2:24 calls preachers to be "kind to everyone." I've looked, but there's no asterisk in the text indicating exceptions to the rule. So "everyone" must include the lady in the third row with crossed arms and an angry countenance. "Everyone" includes the guy who has pledged to fight you every step of the way.

Practically speaking, showing kindness means we smile and look people in the eye as we preach, even if some avoid eye contact. We may not see eye to eye with everyone, but we should be able to look everyone in the eye. Showing kindness also means we actively take steps to restore strained relationships. We do everything we can to follow the admonition in Romans 12:18: "If possible, so far as it depends on you, live peaceably with all."

Winsomely present truth. Even in the face of opposition, a preacher must be "able to teach ... correcting his opponents with gentleness" (2 Timothy 2:24). Kindness should not be equated with weakness. Gentleness is no excuse for cowardice. We must always teach God's truth—but in a courageous, gracious, and winsome way. We must make sure our hearts are in sync with the Spirit—having put off all "bitterness and wrath and anger and clamor and slander ... along with all malice" (Ephesians 4:31)— and then preach God's truth without apology or compromise.

Trust God to change hearts. A big reason we can respond to the disgruntled in a gracious way comes from knowing that changing hearts is ultimately God's job, not ours. As Paul reminds Timothy, "God may perhaps grant them repentance leading to a knowledge of the truth" (2 Timothy 2:25). We can present truth, but only God can bring someone to the knowledge of the truth. This insight takes a great deal of pressure off us as preachers. It frees us up to preach joyfully even when some in the congregation are disgruntled.

The dozing and disgruntled still show up at most churches. Expect them. Even when you are winsome in your preaching, you will win some and lose some when it comes to engaging the disengaged. By preaching God's Word in a courageous and kind way—by speaking the truth in love—you will fulfill your calling and give the disengaged an opportunity to reengage with God's truth.

12
BLUE MONDAYS

Ever heard of "Blue Mondays"? My dad, who served as a pastor for over forty years, introduced me to the phrase. Even if you've never heard the term, if you are a preacher, I'm quite sure you can figure out what it means. And I imagine you can see why dealing with Blue Mondays qualifies as one of the tests of a preacher's heart.

While many occupations have a version of Blue Mondays, preachers are especially vulnerable. Some Mondays we wake up rejoicing in the sense of God's presence and goodness we experienced the previous day; other Mondays—not so much.

In some ways, Blue Mondays shouldn't come as a big surprise. Having just expended a great deal of spiritual, emotional, and physical energy on Sunday, we can come into Monday on the backend of an adrenaline rush, perfectly positioned for a let-down. Dr. Archibald Hart, in his book *Adrenaline and Stress*, tells readers to anticipate a need for "recovery time" after high levels of ministry exertion.[1] Blue Mondays can be times when a depleted soul is catching its breath.

But fatigue is not the only reason our hearts can be overcast or downcast on Monday morning. Sometimes depletion is compounded with disappointment. Sunday's sermon didn't go well in spite of our preparation. Maybe we felt flat as we preached. Maybe a critical comment flattened us right after we finished the sermon. I remember a Good Friday message I gave from Isaiah 53. As I stepped off the platform after the closing prayer, a man walked up and said, "You missed it!" He went on to point out a key Hebrew word in the text I failed to emphasize. His words felt like a slap. Sure, it was only a verbal slap and nothing like the physical pummeling Christ endured on the first Good Friday. Still, I went home feeling the sting of his words.

Less dramatic, but almost as deflating, are the Sundays your sermon is met, not with a critique, but only with silence. As you greet people in the lobby, not a single conversation remotely relates to anything just preached. "Pastor, where do we get permission slips for the youth retreat?" someone asks. "Did you know there are no paper towels in the men's restroom?"

---

1. Archibald Hart, *Adrenaline and Stress* (Nashville: Thomas Nelson, 1995), 131.

FAINTING FITS AND
INNER DISQUIETUDE

Charles Spurgeon, the Prince of Preachers, was mightily used by God on countless Sundays. But he still knew all about Blue Mondays. In *Lectures to My Students*, he talks candidly to younger preachers about what he calls "the minister's fainting fits." Spurgeon lists almost a dozen reasons for these low times, including physical maladies, mental exhaustion, sedentary habits, unbroken labor, and personal attacks. He warns us that occasional fainting fits are an occupational hazard for preachers. "After pouring out our souls over our congregations, we feel like empty earthen pitchers which a child might break."[2]

Dietrich Bonhoeffer echoed Spurgeon's sentiments in lectures he gave his students at Finkenwalde Seminary in 1936. He not only taught them how to prepare a sermon; he also instructed them how to prepare for the moments immediately after the sermon. Bonhoeffer knew that, after preaching a sermon, "the pastor himself is in need of pastoral care." He spoke of the inner "disquietude" preachers sometimes experience as they wonder whether "God's word was audible" in their sermon. He warned about the "meaningless conversations that merely cover over that disquietude" or the way a pastor can "become anxious about the opinions that others might have of his sermon."[3]

---

2. Charles Spurgeon, *Lectures to My Students* (Grand Rapids: Zondervan, 1972), 156.

3. Dietrich Bonhoeffer, *Theological Education at Finkenwalde: 1935–1937*, ed. Victoria J. Barnett and Barbara Wojhoski, trans. Douglas W. Stott, vol. 14, Dietrich Bonhoeffer Works (Minneapolis: Fortress Press, 2013), 508.

While I'm not sure I've ever used the word "disquietude," I've experienced what Bonhoeffer is describing. Sometimes after a Sunday service I feel an inner emptiness and restlessness. Even though I tried to preach with earnestness and energy, I had no sense of the Spirit's power at work. As I leave the parking lot, my soul is troubled with the uneasy sense my message didn't connect with my hearers. I remind myself that my identity is found in my union with Christ rather than my performance as a preacher. But the inner ache lingers as a disquieting Sunday turns into a Blue Monday.

Singing the blues on the occasional Monday is something all preachers experience. Everyone has a bad day once in a while. Things get darker, however, when Blue Mondays don't occur only once in a blue moon. And the problem goes deeper still when Blue Mondays don't stay confined to Mondays. When they stop being occasional and become ongoing, when every day is tinged blue, then disquietude moves to discouragement and disillusionment.

JOHN THE BAPTIST AND THE BLUES

One preacher who lived through a blue season was John the Baptist. Locked up by Herod Antipas for fearlessly proclaiming God's convicting truth, he languished in prison and began to lose hope. His preaching ministry had been shut down. Herod continued to rule like a tyrant. Rome continued to crush Israel under its imperial boot. Worse yet, Jesus didn't seem in a hurry to intervene and rectify the situation. In fact, Jesus wasn't living up to the expectations John—and many others—had for the Messiah. In his perplexity, John sent several of his followers to ask Jesus a stark question: "Are you the one who is to come, or shall we look for another?" (Matthew 11:3).

John's question reveals how badly his faith in Jesus had been shaken. This is surprising in light of all we know about him. John was no "reed shaken by the wind" (11:5–7). He would not bend or bow to religious or political pressure. Rarely do we meet someone in Scripture who seems as unshakable as John the Baptist.

Beyond his rugged, leathery persona, John also had supernatural reasons for a sturdy faith in Jesus as God's Messiah. His parents must have told him the story of Jesus' miraculous birth. He had personally witnessed heaven's endorsement when he baptized Jesus in the Jordan river (Matthew 3:16–17). At one time, John had been so sure of Jesus' identity, he heralded him as "the Lamb of God who takes away the sin of the world" (John 1:29). But now, John found himself imprisoned by doubts, discouragement, and desperation. Talk about a Blue Monday.

I find Jesus' response to John's faltering faith incredibly consoling. He sends a message to John—but not the message we might have expected. Jesus doesn't say, "Go and tell John that I'm deeply disappointed in him," or "Go and tell John to get a grip on his faith." Rather than castigate John for his questions, Jesus reinforces his wobbly faith. He reminds John he was currently doing the messianic works predicted by Isaiah: "Go and tell John what you hear and see: the blind receive their sight and the lame walk, lepers are cleansed and the deaf hear, and the dead are raised up, and the poor have good news preached to them. And blessed is the one who is not offended by me" (Matthew 11:4–6).

Jesus doesn't stop there. He gives a strong, public commendation of John and his ministry: "Truly, I say to you, among those born of women, there has arisen no one greater than John the Baptist" (11:11). John may have become disillusioned with Jesus, but Jesus was not disillusioned with John.

DEALING WITH BLUE MONDAYS

So what should we do when our Mondays turn blue?

First, don't be overly surprised by Blue Mondays. They are a regular test of a preacher's heart. Spurgeon wisely reminds us: "The lesson of wisdom is, be not dismayed by soul-trouble. Count it no strange thing, but a part of ordinary ministerial experience."[4] If Spurgeon, and other faithful preachers, found dark days "part of ordinary ministerial experience," we should not expect immunity. Rather, we should see ourselves in good company.

Second, realize God uses Blue Mondays for good in the lives of his preachers. They keep us humble and remind us that—to borrow a line from Rich Mullins—"we are not as strong as we think we are."[5] Charles Spurgeon came to see his fainting fits, not as a punishment, but as a protection: "My witness is, that those who are honoured of their Lord in public have usually to endure a secret chastening, or to carry a peculiar cross, lest

4. Spurgeon, *Lectures to My Students*, 164.

5. Rich Mullins, "We Are Not as Strong as We Think We Are," *Songs* (Nashville: Reunion, 1996).

by any means they exalt themselves and fall into the snare of the devil."[6]

Finally, we should follow the lead of John the Baptist and bring our doubts and disappointments to Jesus. Like John, we will find in him a compassionate Savior who speaks grace and truth into our souls. And not just on Monday but on every day of the week.

_____

6. Spurgeon, *Lectures to My Students*, 164.

13

FAILURE

"Therefore, my beloved brothers, be steadfast, immovable, always abounding in the work of the Lord, knowing that in the Lord your labor is not in vain" (1 Corinthians 15:58). These words, written by the apostle Paul, provide strong encouragement for all who serve the Lord: "Your labor is not in vain."

But for those of us who are called to preach, it doesn't always feel that way. Sometimes it seems our efforts *are* in vain. Week after week, we labor to prepare messages from God's Word. Sunday after Sunday, we stand and deliver the message with all we've got. But month after month, we don't see the transformative changes we hope for. Instead, we see the same rough edges in the lives of people. Our congregation resembles a construction site with more problems than progress.

What should a preacher do when it seems his preaching efforts are in vain? How do we stay steadfast and immovable in the work of the Lord when our hearts are tested and we are tempted to write ourselves off as failures? I've found it helpful to take a closer look at 1 Corinthians 15:58, especially its historical and literary context.

PROBLEMS IN CORINTH

The church in Corinth would have discouraged any preacher. Paul planted the church on his second missionary journey, spending "a year and a half, teaching the word of God among them" (Acts 18:11). He worked hard; in fact, Paul reminded the Corinthians that, by God's grace, he had "worked harder" than anyone else (1 Corinthians 15:10). When it came to "abounding in the work of the Lord," Paul practiced what he preached.

But in spite of his pastoring and preaching, the church in Corinth struggled to grow up in Christ. Located in a brazenly decadent city, the spiritual sewage from the town backed up into the church. Paul's letters to the church address a host of current congregational problems: interpersonal divisions, sexual immorality, embarrassing lawsuits, and theological confusion.

If you were in Paul's place, you might have concluded your ministry labors had been in vain, that all the time and effort you put into teaching and preaching God's Word had been wasted. But that wasn't Paul's conclusion. In spite of all the brokenness and waywardness in the church, Paul never lost confidence. He remained convinced his labors in the Lord were not in vain.

Paul's example should encourage us. When we get a bit gloomy because of the sin that abounds in the place we serve, we should remember what Paul dealt with in the city of Corinth. When we feel overwhelmed by people problems and spiritual challenges in our congregation, we can be thankful we don't have to trade places with Paul. If he could remain confident his work was not in vain, we can too.

THE RESURRECTION CHAPTER

I have a calligraphed rendition of 1 Corinthians 15:58 framed and hung in my office. Like many of my ministry colleagues, I find this verse inspires me for service. But while 1 Corinthians 15:58 has great impact by itself, it carries far more weight when taken in context. After all, this verse wraps up Paul's argument in chapter 15. And the dominant theme of 1 Corinthians 15 can be summed up in one word: resurrection.

If 1 Corinthians 13 can be called the "love chapter," 1 Corinthians 15 should be labeled the "resurrection chapter." The words "raised" or "resurrection" occur over fifteen times. The chapter begins with a reminder that resurrection is central to the gospel message (15:1–3). Then Paul provides an extended explanation and defense for the reality of the believer's bodily resurrection. As Christ was physically raised to a glorified body, so Christians will also be resurrected to glorified bodies. His resurrection assures ours!

Paul wraps up his teaching on resurrection by calling believers to live out their gratitude in lives of faithful service: "Therefore, my brothers, be steadfast, immovable, always abounding in the work of the Lord" (15:58). In context, the command to be steadfast and immovable means standing firm about the reality of the resurrection. If Christians hope to serve well in ministry, they must stand firm about the resurrection.

Paul understands an important ministry principle: if we lose our expectation of resurrection, we may lose our motivation for ministry. If there's no resurrection—if this life is all you get—why spend yourself in ministry? Why not find an easier way to earn a living? If you aren't going to live for eternity, you might as well live for the weekend. As Paul puts it, "If the dead are not raised, 'Let us eat and drink, for tomorrow we die'" (15:32).

On the other hand, when you realize this life is only the first, short chapter of your eternal story, everything changes. You now have good reason to live with an eternal perspective and give yourself fully to the work of the Lord—even when you find yourself pastoring the first church of Corinth; even when ministry gets messy.

Because of the reality of resurrection, we can share Paul's confidence that our labor in the Lord is not in vain. In fact, because of the resurrection, we can actually expect great gain—for others and for ourselves.

ETERNAL GAIN

While it may not always be apparent, our ministry brings eternal gain to the Christians we serve. Paul held to this truth as he labored with the Corinthian Christians. Though they were often more worldly than godly (1 Corinthians 3:3), he refused to give up on them. In spite of disappointments and setbacks, he remained confident God was still at work. He continued teaching God's truth—both in person and in print. He fixed his gaze on a glorious future when believers would be transformed into the likeness of Christ: "We shall also bear the image of the man of heaven" (1 Corinthians 15:49).

In those seasons when it seems our preaching has little impact on the Christians in our congregations, we must hang on to Paul's perspective. One day, in the resurrection, we will see these believers fully transformed into the image of Christ. We will have the joy of knowing God used our preaching and teaching of his Word as part of the transformation process. The glories of resurrection will reveal our work was not in vain. It brought eternal gain to other believers.

Not only will our service bring eternal gain for others, it will bring great reward to us as well. Earlier in his Letter to the Corinthians, Paul spoke of a coming "Day" when faithful ministry would be evaluated and rewarded by Christ (1 Corinthians 3:13–14). The "Day" he anticipated was the day of the Lord—when Christ would return to reign and when believers would be resurrected to inherit the kingdom of God. "Then each one will receive his commendation from God" (1 Corinthians 4:5).

Paul endured being dismissed and disrespected by some in the church because he anticipated the commendation he would receive from Christ. His resurrection perspective shaped his approach to ministry. It gave him confidence that his labor in the Lord was not in vain. Rather, it would bring him eternal gain.

STEADFAST, IMMOVABLE, ABOUNDING

First Corinthians 15:58 still moves me deeply. It stirs my soul by enlarging my perspective. For the past three decades, God has used this verse to motivate me in ministry. It has helped keep my heart steadfast when I was badly shaken. It has spurred me to abound in the work of the Lord when I felt like quitting. It has inspired me to keep preaching God's Word in season and out of season.

I pray the truth of 1 Corinthians 15:58 would move you as well. When your heart is tested by the feeling that you are failing or not seeing the progress you would like, let it move you to stay immoveable, always abounding in the work of the Lord, knowing that in the Lord your labor is not in vain.

14
PAIN

Athletes know all about playing hurt. For preachers, it's preaching hurt—preaching in pain. Preach for any length of time and you'll face the challenge of preaching in pain. It's one of the unavoidable tests of a preacher's heart.

Sunday comes each week whether we are ready or not; whether we are reeling or not. Sometimes the pain we carry may be physical—an illness that impacts the body. More often it will be emotional—affliction that affects the soul. The pain may result from a Sunday morning blow-up at home with a spouse or teenager. Or from seeing a disgruntled church leader, sitting with a scowl and crossed arms as we stand to preach. The pain may come from recent sins that, in spite of being confessed to God, still leave us feeling like pastoral imposters and spiritual poseurs. Pain can come from the cumulative weight we carry as we shepherd people through severe trials.

In spite of the aching in our souls, when the final song of the worship set finishes, we are expected to stand and deliver. We make our way to the front with an unseen limp, feeling numb, flatlined, or defeated before we even begin. We silently cry out to God for help. We pray that God would make his strength perfect in our weakness. Then we try to preach in pain.

As I reflect on my years of preaching, I still carry some scorched memories of several Sundays when I wasn't sure I would be able to make it through the message. As the opening songs launched the service, I was physically present but emotionally absent. I was vaguely aware of voices around me singing praise to God as I silently voiced my own pain to God. Though preaching has been one of the great joys of my life, on those Sundays, preaching was the last thing I felt like doing. Empty and aching, I called out to God for mercy and help.

The apostle Paul was no stranger to preaching in pain. When he wrote to the church in Corinth, he reminded them of that reality: "And I was with you in weakness and in fear and much trembling" (1 Corinthians 2:3). He expressed a similar thought in his Letter to the Thessalonians: "But though we had already suffered and been shamefully treated at Philippi, as you know, we had boldness in our God to declare to you the gospel of God in the midst of much conflict" (1 Thessalonians 2:2). In both

Corinth and Thessalonica—in spite of the pain he was living with—Paul opened his heart and mouth to proclaim God's message. Clearly, Paul knew how to preach hurt.

As I hear Paul's candid testimony, I long to be able to ask him some questions. How did you do it? What kept you from giving up or calling it quits? Did you ever feel disingenuous talking to others about God's goodness and grace when life and ministry were excruciatingly difficult? How did you quiet the inner turmoil in your own soul enough to concentrate on ministering to the souls of others?

While we can't converse with Paul, we can discern his answers to these questions by taking a closer look at his words in both 1 Corinthians 2 and 1 Thessalonians 2. In these two chapters, we learn at least four important lessons about preaching in pain.

IT'S PART OF FAITHFUL GOSPEL MINISTRY

Paul didn't see personal pain as a reason to cease and desist from proclaiming God's truth. Carrying the scars of a recent beating in Philippi (Acts 16:22) and facing stiff opposition in Thessalonica, he still had the boldness to proclaim the gospel in the local synagogue (Acts 17:2).

From Paul's example we learn that a faithful preaching ministry will, at times, call for a determined, daring spirit that speaks in spite of personal pain. At those moments, our preaching becomes an act of defiance against the darkness. Though sorrow may hang overcast in our hearts, we continue to proclaim the truth that the sun is shining above the clouds. In these moments, we join Paul in become daring preachers who don't play it safe or run for cover when ministry gets painful.

So on those Sundays when pain obscures the joy of preaching God's Word, we endure hardship and soldier on (2 Timothy 2:3–4). We report for duty even when we aren't as healthy or happy as we'd like to be. We preach God's Word, in season and out of season, on good days and hard days.

IT INVOLVES SPEAKING IN SPITE OF TURBULENT EMOTIONS

As Paul arrived in Corinth, he came "in weakness and in fear and much trembling" (1 Corinthians 2:3). But in spite of turbulent emotions that left him feeling rattled, he still proclaimed "the testimony of God" (2:1). While he was aware of his feelings, he wasn't silenced by them.

Paul's candid comments provide a helpful reminder that we can preach even when our inner world is not placid and peaceful. The internal turbulence caused by weakness, fear, and trembling do not disqualify us as preachers. Faithfulness in preaching sometimes involves preaching when we are badly shaken. While we may not be able to publicly explain our pain, we can publicly proclaim God's truth.

Mature preachers don't ignore or deny their emotions. Instead, they pour out their hearts to God in private (Psalm 62:8) and proclaim his Word in public (1 Corinthians 2:1). While they may openly acknowledge something of their weakness and need for God's enabling grace, they don't focus attention on themselves; rather, they point people to Christ. They follow Paul's lead and resolve "to know nothing ... except Jesus Christ" (2:2).

IT'S NOT AN EXCUSE FOR SINFUL ATTITUDES OR ACTIONS

As I read Paul's reflection on his preaching ministry, I'm struck by how he maintained his spiritual integrity even when mistreated in ministry. He didn't allow painful experiences to become an excuse for sinful attitudes or actions.

He examined his motives and his message to make sure his preaching was not fueled by "error or impurity or any attempt to deceive" (1 Thessalonians 2:3). Paul understood the difference between preaching in distress and preaching in disguise. Though he was still banged up from the abuse he'd received in Philippi and surely would have welcomed some encouraging words, he still didn't look for praise from his hearers (2:4). Instead, he proclaimed God's truth with integrity, seeking to please the One who "tests our hearts" (2:4).

Here is an important reminder for all of us who preach, especially when life and ministry are painful. The mistreatment we experience must not be allowed to muddy our motives or pollute our message. We can't allow bitterness over past hurts to color our present sermons. We must not let pain prompt us to change God's message for our own gain (2:5) or glory (2:6). We must stay mindful of the truth that God is the One who examines our work. We will make it our first priority to live and preach for his approval. While life may not be going well, we will seek to make sure it is well with our souls.

IT MAKES US LEAN HARDER ON THE POWER OF GOD

Paul's example, though inspiring on one level, can be deflating on another. Spiritually sensitive preachers who know their own sinful hearts can read Paul's testimony and respond by piling more pain on their own souls. We can beat ourselves up for responding poorly when we were beaten up in ministry. We can readily recall times we allowed ministry wounds to fester in our hearts and infect our sermons. We are painfully aware that responding well to painful circumstances doesn't come easily or automatically.

The same was true for Paul. While we may think Paul handled mistreatment effortlessly, a close reading of his words dispels that illusion. Paul points the Thessalonians to the source of his strength in times of great weakness: "We had boldness in our God to declare to you the gospel of God in the midst of much conflict" (2:2). The strength to be bold when he was banged up came from God, not from within himself.

Paul told the Corinthian Christians the same thing. When preaching in "weakness and in fear and much trembling," he relied on the "demonstration of the Spirit and of power, so that your faith might not rest in the wisdom of men but the power of God" (1 Corinthians 2:3–5).

Preaching in pain has a purpose—both in the life of the preacher and the hearers. Pain has a way of driving us as preachers to a greater dependence on God's Spirit. We become more realistic about ourselves and more reliant on God's power. Pain also has a beneficial effect on our hearers. They see a living demonstration of the truth that faith must rest on God rather than his messengers (2:5).

So on Sundays when we don't feel like preaching because we're in pain—when we feel empty and broken—we can actually do some of our best work as preachers. That's because we will be more conscious of our need of God's grace and more dependent on his Spirit's power. And when God chooses to work through our weakness, we will be less apt to embezzle his glory. Like Paul, we come to understand in a very personal way that "when I am weak, then I am strong" (2 Corinthians 12:10).

15
QUITTING

The prophet Jeremiah wasn't a quitter, but there were days he wanted to quit. Read what he lived through over the course of his forty-year ministry and you will understand why he wanted to resign. God gave him one of the toughest ministry assignments ever. The people and leaders of Judah routinely ridiculed his messages. Family members and friends from his hometown of Anathoth plotted to kill him. He was brutally beaten up and imprisoned at the bottom of a filthy cistern. He lived through the siege and destruction of Jerusalem. Near the end of his life he was force-marched to Egypt where, as best we can tell, he died in exile. No wonder he's called the "weeping prophet." No wonder he wanted to quit.

I'm embarrassed to compare the hardships I've faced as a preacher with those Jeremiah endured as a prophet. My troubles in ministry seem lightweight compared to his woes. Even so, my troubles have felt crushing to me at times. Like Jeremiah, I've had days when I wanted to call it quits.

I hit a point where my heart was tempted to quit early in my years as a pastor. Ministry had taken a high toll on my family and on me. I was worn down by turmoil at church and tension at home. So I bought a newspaper, opened up the classified section, and began looking at painting jobs—anything that would put bread on the table and take pressure off my soul. While I didn't consider walking away from my faith or my family, I was ready to walk away from ministry.

PRAYING WITH JEREMIAH

Maybe that's why I appreciate Jeremiah's prayer about quitting. This prayer, recorded in the twentieth chapter of his book, reads like a verbal resignation letter. Jeremiah pours out his battered soul in hot and angry words. He complains about being pummeled for preaching God's Word. He tells the Lord he's ready to resign.

I suspect many pastors reading this have prayed a similar prayer of resignation. While at least one recent study has shown that, contrary to popular belief, most pastors are not quitters,[1] many of us will have days when we feel like quitting.

---

1. A study conducted by LifeWay Research in 2016 challenges the prevailing thinking that pastors are leaving the ministry at an epidemic rate. LifeWay's research of 1,500 evangelical and historic black churches found that only

In fact, the temptation to quit is one of the tests of a preacher's heart. On those Blue Mondays when we feel ready to resign, we can steady and strengthen our souls as we read (and re-read) Jeremiah's resignation prayer.

> O LORD, you have deceived me
>> and I was deceived;
> you are stronger than I,
>> and you have prevailed.
> I have become a laughingstock all the day;
>> everyone mocks me.
> For whenever I speak, I cry out,
>> I shout, "Violence and destruction!"
> For the word of the LORD has become for me
>> a reproach and derision all day long.
>> (Jeremiah 20:7–8)

Strong words, aren't they? Honestly, I would not have had the boldness to speak them out loud or write them down for others to read. Jeremiah essentially accuses God of tricking him into ministry. The Hebrew word for "deceive" means to entice, allure, or fool. Jeremiah says God signed him up for service without disclosing how hard it would be. He wasn't happy with the message he was given to deliver ("Violence and destruction") or the ridicule that came his way ("I have become a laughingstock all the day; everyone mocks me").

---

1 percent of pastors leave the ministry annually. Mark Dance, "Pastors Are Not Quitting in Droves," September 28, 2016, https://factsandtrends.net/2016/09/28/pastors-are-not-quitting-in-droves/.

Preachers whose hearts are tempted to quit often share Jeremiah's disillusionment with their calling—and sometimes with the God who called them into service. Where was the full-disclosure statement about the high cost of ministry? How can God expect anyone to put up with the garbage and grief that comes with pastoring and preaching?

FEELINGS VERSUS FACTS

While Jeremiah's words about being tricked into service accurately picture his feelings, they don't accurately represent the facts. God had not deceived him about how hard his ministry would be. In fact, God spelled things out rather clearly when he called Jeremiah into service: "They will fight against you, but they shall not prevail against you, for I am with you, declares the LORD, to deliver you" (Jeremiah 1:19). Jeremiah would be attacked; his ministry would be a fight.

As pastors, we too must acknowledge God didn't camouflage the cost when calling us into ministry. We've read Jesus' warning to expect hostility (John 15:18) and Paul's admonition to soldier up (2 Timothy 2:3–4). Still, there are times when we feel the cost is more than we can afford to pay. While we don't want to be a quitter, at times—like Jeremiah—we want to quit.

But quitting isn't as easy as it sounds. Listen to Jeremiah's dilemma as he tries to resign. "If I say, 'I will not mention him, or speak anymore in his name,' there is in my heart as it were a burning fire shut up in my bones, and I am weary with holding it in, and I cannot" (Jeremiah 20:9). Every time Jeremiah decides to stop preaching God's message, a fire starts burning inside him. He can't extinguish or smother it no matter how hard he tries.

Have you ever forgotten to open the flue after lighting a fire in your fireplace? The smoke that billows into the room gets your attention in a hurry. As Jeremiah contemplates quitting, his soul becomes a fireplace with the flue shut. No matter how he tries, he can't smother the fiery passion that burns inside him. He can't stay silent for long.

If you've been called to preach, you understand Jeremiah's dilemma. God's Word is a fire in your bones. Like Paul, you find yourself saying, "Woe to me if I do not preach the gospel" (1 Corinthians 9:16). One of the evidences of a call to the ministry of preaching is the unshakeable, unquenchable internal pressure to proclaim God's Word. Even when you want to quit.

The fact that Jeremiah can't seem to quit doesn't stop his lament. As you read the rest of his prayer, you hear him continue to complain about the lousy treatment he's receiving: people whispering behind his back; people watching for him to make a misstep (Jeremiah 20:10). All of a sudden, for a brief, shining moment, he regains hope that God will deliver him (20:11–13). Just as quickly, he descends again into a dark place. In fact, he finishes his jeremiad by wishing he had never been born (20:14–18).

LEARNING FROM JEREMIAH

What lessons should we learn from Jeremiah's prayer and his desire to quit? Are we to conclude that the call to preach comes with a fire in our bones that never dies out? Does "once a preacher" mean "always a preacher"? Is quitting sinning? Answering these questions, especially for a preacher feeling Jeremiah's pain and confusion, requires both careful thought and a caring heart. Some in pastoral ministry will not always remain in vocational service but will live out their calling to preach in other settings (for example, in my case, as a seminary professor). Still, all of us with a God-given passion to preach can find hope and help from Jeremiah's example. Let me boldface three biblical truths from Jeremiah's life that have encouraged me as a preacher in my Jeremiah moments.

God allows preachers to vent their desire to quit in a full-strength, undiluted way. While we must never lose our high and holy reverence for God, we are given freedom to pour out our hearts to God in prayer. Had I been asked to edit Jeremiah's prayer before it went to press, I would have told him to tone down his rhetoric and sanitize his sentiments. Amazingly, God didn't do that. Here is great consolation for our souls. Our gracious God and Father lets us speak honestly about the realities of ministry even when our perspectives get distorted by pain.

The passion to preach God's Word is a fire not easily extinguished. Even when Jeremiah felt burned by ministry, God's Word still burned in his bones. Even when he determined to stop speaking "in his name," the fire continued to blaze. His complaints couldn't smother it. His tears couldn't douse it.

I am one of many preachers who have lived the truth of Jeremiah's words. I have felt scorched in ministry, ready to stop speaking in his name. But the fire has continued to burn. Sometimes my passion to preach has been reduced to embers; more often it has blazed in full flame. I'm grateful the calling to preach God's Word is fired by a God-given desire not easily extinguished.

The God who starts us as preachers sustains us as preachers. Though Jeremiah thought he was finished preaching, God was not finished with Jeremiah. When God first called Jeremiah, he made him a promise. Not a promise to shield him from trouble, but to support and sustain him through trouble: "They will fight against you, but they shall not prevail against you, for I am with you, declares the LORD, to deliver you" (Jeremiah 1:19). Over the long, difficult years that followed, God kept his promise.

While I've not preached as long as Jeremiah or experienced anything approaching his trauma, I have known the same grace that sustained him in ministry. When I was ready to quit— when painting seemed preferable to preaching—God's presence and mercy sustained me. His Word both comforted my soul and toughened it up. In subtle and sometimes stunning ways, he changed my situation or provided enough support to keep me going and renew my hope. I'm deeply thankful God listens to our prayers when we feel like quitting. Even more, I'm thankful his sustaining grace never quits on us.

PART II
THE STRENGTHENING
OF A PREACHER'S HEART

"Keep your heart with all vigilance for
from it flow the springs of life."

Proverbs 4:23

As preachers, we will have our hearts tested. Like it or not. Ready or not. In part I, we considered fifteen heart-level tests we can expect to face. Some of these tests are highly predictable; we can anticipate them. Others will come as a surprise, ambushing us at unexpected moments. All of them call us to take Proverbs 4:23 to heart and keep our hearts with all vigilance.

When we talk about guarding or keeping our hearts, we may only think of playing defense, fending off the temptations that threaten to trip us up or take us down. But keeping our hearts requires more than being reactive; we must also become proactive. We must not only play defense; we need to go on the offense. We must intentionally fortify our hearts, strengthening our souls for the tests that most certainly will come our way.

In part II, the focus shifts from being reactive to becoming more proactive. Instead of concentrating on how to respond well when our hearts get tested, we'll consider how to prepare in advance for future tests. In the following ten chapters, I highlight specific ways we can actively strengthen our souls as preachers.

16

PRACTICE
PERSONAL SOUL CARE

In my first year of university, I majored in music with an emphasis on voice. I quickly learned I didn't have what it takes to be a premier vocalist. First, there was the small matter of talent. Or more accurately, the lack of it. I lacked the raw abilities that could be refined into something musically sublime. But there was another problem. I wasn't ready to commit to the rigors of keeping my vocal cords in top shape.

My voice teacher viewed her vocal cords as a fine instrument, the vocal equivalent of a vintage Stradivarius. She understood if she damaged her instrument, she would not produce vocally. If her throat became sore, she couldn't soar. So she made commitments she saw as both logical and necessary. They struck me as austere and extreme. For starters, she wouldn't have lunch in the school cafeteria. It was way too noisy, causing her to strain her voice to hold a conversation. As a result, she refused to join other students or faculty for lunch.

If keeping your voice in top condition ranks as a top priority, you will want to dine in peace and quiet. As an eighteen-year-old, I wasn't about to skip lunch in the cafeteria or sit there silently just to protect my vocal cords. That seemed unnatural, even draconian. At the end of my first year of university, I switched my major from music to ministry.

Over the years, I've gained a better appreciation for my voice teacher's outlook and actions. I've come to see her extreme efforts to protect her voice as a practical expression of her desire to produce beautiful music.

As a preacher, I have a primary instrument as well, and it's not my voice. My primary instrument as a preacher is my soul—the non-physical part of my being that has the job of capturing and conveying the message of God's Word. My soul is my Stradivarius, the instrument God has given me to give voice to his gospel.

Since the Bible's use of "soul" and "heart" shows a good deal of semantic overlap, I view personal soul care as an essential part of guarding my heart.[1] Like my voice teacher, I must keep

---

1. According to the *Eerdmans Bible Dictionary*, "soul" is "the usual translation of Heb. *nepeš* and Gk. *psyché* (though most translations retain considerable freedom in their renderings of these terms). As with other terms such as

my soul—my instrument—in good shape or I will be a poor preacher, unable to play the music of the gospel in a clear, compelling manner. To better care for my own soul, I've made four commitments that, together, help keep my soul in good shape for preaching.

CULTIVATE A DEVOTIONAL LIFE BIGGER THAN MY SERMON PREPARATION

My sermon preparation necessarily gets me into the Word of God. What a delight! Can you believe we preachers get paid to study God's Word? Many weeks, the biblical study I do for sermon preparation is spiritually enriching for my soul. God's Word begins its work in me—I'm the first hearer of the message.

Having said that, I have found it important to have a devotional life in the Scripture that is larger than my sermon preparation. So I begin each morning reading a passage in Scripture I'm not studying for a message. I come to God's Word to hear his message to me, not to get a message for others. I come as one of his sheep, not one of his shepherds. Sometimes what I glean in this time will later make its way into a sermon, but that's not the focus.

'body,' 'heart,' and 'spirit,' 'soul' does not designate a part of a human being, but rather the whole person considered from one particular aspect of its functioning. As such, it represents primarily the life force of the body (cf. Gen. 2:7) or the inner life of the person, encompassing desires and emotions." "Soul," in *Eerdmans Bible Dictionary*, ed. Allen C. Myers (Grand Rapids: Eerdmans, 1987), 964.

I fear that without regular time in God's Word separate from sermon preparation, I might gradually become a "professional Christian." I could develop a utilitarian approach to God's Word—seeing the Bible only as a tool for getting sermons ready to preach.

To protect my soul against coming to Scripture only for work and not worship, I need unhurried time to linger in God's presence, listening very personally to his voice as it comes to me through his Word. Here I commune with God in secret. Here my soul is shaped in private ways that ultimately show up in the public arena of life and ministry.

GET MY SOUL HAPPY IN GOD

George Müller, who lived a busy life leading an orphanage and preaching the gospel, started each day with the conviction that his "first great and primary business" was to have his soul "happy in God."[2] Müller was on to something important. If our souls are not finding joy and satisfaction in God, they become thin and brittle, lacking vitality and resiliency. On the other hand, when our souls are "filled with all the fullness of God" (Ephesians 3:19), we are able to preach out of the overflow. Our confidence and contentment in God color the way we communicate. While we remain serious about God's Word, we are less prone to become somber and heavy. The joy in our souls bubbles up in our sermons.

---

2. John Piper, "George Mueller's Strategy for Showing God," 2004 Bethlehem Conference for Pastors, February 3, 2004, www.desiringgod.org/messages/george-muellers-strategy-for-showing-god#77.

So how do we get our souls happy in God? Certainly, as Müller discovered, this will involve regular, extended times of saturating our souls in Scripture and strengthening them through prayer. But there's more to it. A satisfied, joyful soul comes as we take time and make space to enjoy the many gifts and graces God grants us: a walk in the woods, a Sunday afternoon nap, the taste of a ripe peach, an evening out with good friends, a getaway to the lake or the beach. As Joe Rigney explains, "God's gifts become avenues for enjoying him, beams of glory that we chase back to the source. We don't set God and his gifts in opposition to each other, as though they are rivals. Instead, in the words of Charles Simeon, we 'enjoy God in everything and everything in God.'"[3]

Getting and keeping our souls happy in God rarely comes easily amidst the pressures and pulls of life and ministry. But like George Müller, we should make it our "first great and primary business." This will mean following the wise counsel Dallas Willard gave to a busy pastor: "Arrange your life so that you are experiencing deep contentment, joy and confidence in your everyday life with God."[4]

AVOID WHATEVER SULLIES MY SOUL

Nothing blunts a preacher's effectiveness like sin—not fatigue, failure, sickness, or suffering. Sin, in any of its manifestations, interrupts fellowship with God and hinders the flow of

---

3. Joe Rigney, *The Things of Earth: Treasuring God by Enjoying His Gifts* (Wheaton, IL: Crossway, 2015), 99.

4. Dallas Willard, *Living in Christ's Presence: Final Words on Heaven and the Kingdom of God* (Downers Grove, IL: InterVarsity Press, 2014), 106.

the Spirit's power through us. What's more, as Sam Storms observes, sin desensitizes us like "spiritual novocaine, numbing one's heart to the horror of self-centeredness and rebellion against God."[5]

Preachers must keep a sensitive heart toward God, allowing his Spirit to quickly alert us when we are tempted to sin or have given way to temptation. I've found this requires staying vigilant, not only to the more overt manifestations of sin, but also to the more covert compromises that sully my soul.

Susanna Wesley—John Wesley's mother—wisely taught her children to see sin as anything that caused them to fall short of the glory of God: "If you would judge the lawfulness or the unlawfulness of pleasure, then take this simple rule: Whatever weakens your reason, impairs the tenderness of your conscience, obscures your sense of God and takes off the relish of spiritual things—that to you is sin."[6]

Remembering Susanna's words has led me to stop reading a best-selling novel because, in order to keep reading, I would have had to silence my conscience. At other times, I've opted to forgo watching a critically acclaimed movie because I knew it would mess with my mind. It has meant pulling away from watching my favorite NFL team because I sensed I had become overly absorbed with their success or failure. I remember a Sunday evening communion service when, as the elements

5. Sam Storms, *Packer on the Christian Life: Knowing God in Christ, Walking by the Spirit* (Wheaton, IL: Crossway, 2015), 96.

6. Charles Wallace, *Susanna Wesley, The Complete Writings* (Oxford: Oxford University Press, 1977), 109.

were being passed, I was rehearsing the plays that cost my team the game. Football was obscuring my sense of God and taking the relish off spiritual things. (Today, I find I can watch my favorite team play and it no longer has the same hold on my heart.)

My point in all this is not to impose personal standards on others. Legalism is both unbiblical and unproductive (Colossians 2:20–23). However, as pastors we must prioritize the maintenance of our spiritual lives in practical, personalized ways.

Some will hear this and chafe. Won't this make us spiritual Luddites, awkwardly out of step with those we are trying to walk alongside of in ministry? Won't we miss out on some of the good things in life? Perhaps. But I would counter with a question: How important is it for you to have your instrument (your soul) in top spiritual condition? If you agree that the condition of your soul is crucial in communicating God's message, then you will commit yourself to avoiding whatever sullies your soul, obscures your sense of God, or takes the relish away from spiritual things.

PREACH THE GOSPEL TO MYSELF EVERY DAY—ESPECIALLY SUNDAYS

No matter how committed we are to walking in humility and holiness, we will stumble at times. It's impossible to walk through this fallen world and not dirty our feet and muddy our souls. Our sense of God will become obscured at times. We will lose our joy in spiritual things. Our souls will not always feel happy in God.

And yet, Sunday comes as scheduled. It comes whether or not our sermons are ready. And it comes whether or not our souls are ready.

If I had to choose, I'd much rather step up to preach with my sermon unfinished than my soul unprepared. Preaching becomes a heavy burden when we cannot honestly sing, "It is well with my soul." Speaking with a sullied soul leaves us feeling like poseurs, not preachers.

That's why preachers must not only preach the gospel to others; we must begin by preaching the gospel to our own souls. On Sundays when our souls are clouded over by grief or guilt, we must preach the gospel to ourselves before we preach it to the congregation. We must not presume upon God's grace, but we still must preach the good news to our own hearts.

As preachers, we are right in seeing personal holiness as a prerequisite for faithful and fruitful proclamation of God's Word. We must constantly heed Paul's instruction to Timothy: "Keep a close watch on yourself and on the teaching. Persist in this, for by so doing you will save both yourself and your hearers" (1 Timothy 4:16). We must be vigilant to pray for spiritual protection as Jesus taught us (Matthew 6:13). We must cooperate with God's Spirit and "put to death the deeds of the body" (Romans 8:13). We must take to heart the admonition from Puritan pastor John Owen: "Be killing sin or it will be killing you."[7] And when we give way to temptation and fall into sin, we must

---

7. John Owen, *On the Mortification of Sin in Believers,* The Works of John Owen 6 (Edinburgh: T&T Clark, 1862), 9.

be quick to respond to the Spirit's conviction, confessing our sins and trusting Christ for cleansing (1 John 1:9). If we are to be "useful to the master" in our ministry as preachers, we must be cleansed and "set apart as holy" (2 Timothy 2:20–21).

The subtle danger for preachers comes when we forget that our usefulness is always based on God's grace. Jerry Bridges wisely reminds us that on our worst days we are not beyond the reach of God's grace and on our best days we are not beyond the need for it.[8] Preaching the gospel to ourselves helps us remember God's grace.

So when our sense of God is obscured by foolish or sinful choices, we must come back to the cross, claiming the gift of forgiveness Christ procured for us through his death and resurrection. When Satan tempts us to believe our sins and failures render us unworthy and unusable to God, we remind ourselves we are forgiven not because of the depth of our sorrows but because of the death of God's Son (Ephesians 1:7). We don't earn our way back into God's good graces. We come boldly, by faith, to find grace and mercy in our time of need (Hebrews 4:14–16). Preachers must preach the gospel—starting with ourselves, especially on Sundays.

Back in my university days, I couldn't grasp why my vocal teacher was so insistent on protecting her vocal cords. Now I get it—not as a singer but as a preacher. As you only get one set of vocal cords, you only get one soul. Personal soul care is

---

8. Jerry Bridges, *The Discipline of Grace* (Colorado Springs: NavPress, 1994), 18.

not a luxury but a necessity for all of us who desire to stay in top form so we can give out the beautiful music of God's Word.

Strengthening our hearts to proclaim God's Word calls for personal soul care. This kind of soul care always involves prayer: we pray to commune with God, keep our souls happy in him, repent of sin, and strengthen our hearts in the gospel of God's grace. But prayer plays an even larger role for us as preachers; we must pray throughout the entire preaching process. To that important topic we turn next.

17
DEVOTE YOURSELF TO PRAYER AND THE WORD

"And he told them a parable to the effect that they ought always to pray and not lose heart" (Luke 18:1). These words reveal the close link between the constancy of our prayers and the condition of our hearts. Failing to pray leads to heart failure. On the other hand, faithfulness in prayer is one of the ways we strengthen our hearts.

God designed prayer to play a central part in our lives. That's true for all Christians, but especially for those of us given the privilege and responsibility of preaching God's Word. Faithful preaching requires devoted praying. The apostles understood this and determined to prioritize prayer alongside preaching:

"We will devote ourselves to prayer and the ministry of the word" (Acts 6:4). God intends preaching and prayer to be intimately joined together. And what God has joined together, let no preacher separate.

But what does it look like for a preacher to remain devoted both to prayer and the Word? How do we make prayer an integral part of the preaching process? How are we to strengthen our souls in prayer so we don't lose heart? I believe the answer lies in integrating prayer throughout the entire preaching process—from start to finish. Here's what that could look like in practice.

BEFORE THE SERMON

Praying about what to preach. Many preachers work through a book of the Bible, or a section of that book. They will often add topical expositions between series or, as needed, within a sermon series.

Praying about the series or specific sermons means waiting on the Lord for ideas or insights regarding what series to plan. Sometimes this internal leading comes as I get away from the office and take intentional time to prayerfully listen to God. Sometimes ideas come unexpectedly in the course of life and ministry. Almost always the choice of what to preach combines my sense of the needs of the congregation and my own interest in the book or topic.

Praying during sermon exegesis. As we study, we should pray that God would grant us the ability to accurately understand the message of the text. We echo the words of King David: "Open my eyes, that I may behold wondrous things out of your law" (Psalm 119:18).

Prayer during exegesis plays out as a running conversation with the Lord. "Father, help me understand how this verse fits the flow of the passage." "What am I missing here?" "Lord, what is the main message of this text?"

In a sense, this is what it means to do sermon study *coram Deo*—before the face of God. We see sermon preparation as a prompt to an ongoing conversation with God about his Word. In this way, sermon preparation becomes part of our own spiritual development.

Praying during sermon development. A primary goal of our study is to come to a clear understanding of the dominant message of the passage—the big idea. But even after we have come to clarity on the major message of the text, we need God's enablement to craft an impactful sermon around that meaning. Here again, we need to pray.

In his book *Deep Preaching*, Kent Edwards gives some helpful instruction to preachers about how to make prayer a more central part of sermon development. Drawing on Jesus' words about entering a private place to pray (Matthew 6:5–6), Edwards encourages preachers to take their exegetical findings into their "prayer closet." He even provides a list of "closet questions" to help preachers prayerfully process the truth of a passage in God's presence.

Edwards was exercised to develop these closet questions after listening to one of his students' sermons in a seminary preaching class. As a homiletic professor, Edwards had to give the sermon an "A" for its well-crafted, technical precision. At the same time, he was troubled; the sermon, while methodologically excellent, was spiritually flat. Edwards says the student "had gazed at the truth of Scripture without being overwhelmed by it. He had held the truth in his hands but, unlike Jeremiah, he had not eaten it. He knew God's Word externally but not internally. The sermon was shallow."[1]

To develop deeper sermons, Edwards calls for preachers to spend time in prayer after they've done their initial exegesis and discovered the big idea of the passage. He encourages them to focus their prayers by looking in five directions:[2]

- Look Backward: "Why was this exegetical idea *necessary* for its original recipients?"
- Look Upward: "What is God revealing about *Himself* in this text?"
- Look Inward: "What is God saying to *me* in this text?"
- Look Outward: "What does God want to *accomplish* in this text?"
- Look Forward: "What could *negate* the progress I have just made through this text?"

---

1. Kent Edwards, *Deep Preaching* (Nashville: B&H Academic, 2009), 2.
2. Edwards, *Deep Preaching*, 187–92.

I've found that taking time to prayerfully work through these questions helps me clarify the purpose and discern the direction the sermon should take. Spending "closet time" talking with God about the implications of a passage prepares me to manuscript a message that is both true to the text of Scripture and helpful to the hearts of my hearers.

Praying before you preach. Praying before the sermon has taken several forms over the course of my years as a preacher. On Saturday night, I often sit down with my manuscript and prayerfully work through it. I seek to listen to God's Spirit, giving him freedom to prompt final changes in what I've prepared. Also on Saturday evening, my wife, Linda, and I kneel by the couch and pray about the upcoming day—including the impact of the sermon.

Some preachers I know take time to walk through the room where they will preach, pausing to pray for those who will sit in the seats. Many preachers gather for prayer with a group of leaders right before the service begins. For many years, I met for prayer with a group of godly men before the Sunday service. These men had committed to pray for me all week; on Sundays they met to pray with me, asking God's Spirit to work through the message to change lives.

DURING AND AFTER THE SERMON

Praying as you preach. As preachers, we tend to see our sermons as delivered to those in the congregation. We sometimes forget our sermons are also offerings given to God. Our sermons are spiritual sacrifices, "the fruit of lips that acknowledge his name" (Hebrews 13:15). We can have a dual conversation going on as we preach. Outwardly, we present the message we've developed to the congregation; inwardly we cry to God for His help. We hold communion with God even as we speak to people. Some of the sweetest and strongest times of sensing God's presence come as we preach God's Word in communion with him.

Praying after you preach. God's evaluation of our sermons is much broader than we often realize. He evaluates how we used our time and energy to prepare to preach. He looks at our motives as we preach. He also examines how we process things once the sermon is over. Do we swell up with pride on days we receive an unusual amount of affirmation? Do we give way to insecurity on days the sermon felt lifeless, when we saw that dreaded glazed look on too many faces?

This is why we must continue to pray even after we finish preaching. Dietrich Bonhoeffer warned seminary students their hearts would be especially vulnerable immediately after they finished preaching.[3] For this reason, we must not only pray as we prepare or as we proclaim God's Word; we must also pray when we finish our sermons. Whether the sermon seemed to soar or sink, we should pray. We carry our buoyant or bruised hearts into God's presence. We offer up praise for the privilege of being a preacher of his Word. We surrender to him the impact (or perceived lack of impact) of the sermon. In short, we

---

3. Dietrich Bonhoeffer, *Theological Education at Finkenwalde: 1935–1937,* ed. Victoria J. Barnett and Barbara Wojhoski, trans. Douglas W. Stott, vol. 14, Dietrich Bonhoeffer Works (Minneapolis, MN: Fortress Press, 2013), 530.

worship by offering up the entire preaching experience—good or bad—to the Lord.

PRAYER AND THE PREACHER'S SOUL

As preachers, we often see preaching as something we do to shape the souls of our listeners. We can forget that God has a bigger agenda: he also uses the preaching process to shape the soul of the preacher. Preaching is not just about communicating God's truth. It's also about communing with the God of truth.

So far in part II, we've focused on spiritual practices (soul care, prayer) that strengthen our souls to proclaim God's Word. Now I want to turn to a heart-level conviction that provides protection and direction as we prepare to preach: setting our hearts to stay on the expository path.

18

STAY ON THE
EXPOSITORY PATH

If you want to strengthen your heart as a preacher, it isn't enough to respond to various tests as they come up. You need to proactively set your heart: "For Ezra had set his heart to study the Law of the LORD, and to do it and to teach his statutes and rules in Israel" (Ezra 7:10). Setting your heart involves establishing core convictions to guide you as a person and as a preacher. These convictions shape how you approach God's Word to study, practice, and teach it. These convictions help stabilize you as a preacher when you face critical feedback or cultural pressure.

A primary, heart-level conviction that will strengthen your soul to proclaim God's Word is the decision to become and remain an expository preacher. The word "expository" is more than a bit fuzzy for many people. Some think being an expository preacher means your sermons are a verbal verse-by-verse commentary on a passage of Scripture. Others assume it means preaching sequentially through Ephesians, Genesis, or another book in the Bible. Some associate exposition with being strong on historical explanation but weak on relevant application. So before making a commitment for or against exposition, a preacher must be clear on what is involved.

HADDON ROBINSON MEETS ROBERT FROST

In his book *Biblical Preaching,* Haddon Robinson, a leading advocate for expository preaching, provides a single, penetrating question to help us determine whether we are committed to expository preaching: "Do you as a preacher endeavor to bend your thoughts to the Scriptures or do you use the Scriptures to support your thoughts?"[1] Expositors bend their thoughts to Scripture; non-expositors do the reverse.

To adapt a line from poet Robert Frost, two roads diverge in the homiletical woods.[2] At this homiletical fork in the road, all preachers must decide which path to follow. The expository path—the road less traveled—follows the text wherever it leads. On the expository path, the Scripture, not the preacher, sets the sermon's direction. The alternative path heads in a

---

1. Haddon Robinson, *Biblical Preaching* (Grand Rapids: Baker Books, 1980), 20.

2. Robert Frost, "The Road Not Taken," Poetry Foundation, www.poetry foundation.org/poems/44272/the-road-not-taken.

direction chosen by the preacher. Scripture may be used on this path, but it's not followed in the same way.

Not everyone champions the expository path as the right one for preachers and audiences. Take Harry Emerson Fosdick, a well-known preacher from the early twentieth century. While some in Fosdick's day advocated expository preaching as the cure for shallow sermons, Fosdick saw it only as the cure for insomnia:

> Many preachers ... indulge habitually in what they call expository sermons. They take passages from Scripture and, proceeding on the assumption that the people attending church that morning are deeply concerned about what the passage means, they spend their half hour or more on historical exposition of the verse or chapter, ending with some appended practical application to the auditors. Could any procedure be more surely predestined to dullness and futility?[3]

So does a commitment to exposition guarantee irrelevant, boring sermons? While anyone can preach a boring sermon, a commitment to exposition doesn't increase the odds. In fact, expository preaching done well not only proves faithful to Scripture but also fascinating to listeners.

---

3. Harry Emerson Fosdick, "What Is the Matter with Preaching?" in Mike Graves, ed., *What's the Matter with Preaching Today?* (Louisville: Westminster John Knox Press, 2004), 9.

WHAT HARRY EMERSON FOSDICK MISSED

Fosdick misunderstood expository preaching, so he missed the major advantages it brings to both preachers and their congregations. Here are just three of the benefits of a commitment to exposition.

1. More authority in your sermons. Preacher, who do you think you are to tell others what to think or do? What gives you the right to impose your ideas on others? Why should anyone listen to you?

Expository preachers answer these questions with a confident humility. We say, "I have no authority in myself to tell anyone what to think or do; but God does. My authority is derived from and dependent upon his Word."

Since the Bible is the Word of God, those who faithfully exposit Scripture speak with God's authority. Only as we accurately expound the Word of God can we honestly claim God's backing for our sermons.

In fact, if we don't ground our preaching squarely on God's Word, we build on some other foundation. It may be our own ideas, prevailing cultural thinking, or the latest scientific or sociological findings. But if it is something other than Scripture, we stand on shifting sand. Only as we preach God's Word can we give people rock-solid truth. Only then do we prepare them to weather the storms of life and the deluge of judgment day (Matthew 7:24–27).

2. More nourishment for your people. Back in Jeremiah's time, the preachers getting the most attention were serving up a steady diet of their own dreams and visions. God assessed these sermons as spiritual junk food. He wanted spokesmen who fed people his Word: "'let him who has my word speak my word faithfully. What has straw in common with wheat?' declares the LORD" (Jeremiah 23:28).

What was true in Jeremiah's day remains true today. To help people grow up spiritually healthy, we must feed them a nourishing diet of God's Word rather than our own dreams and visions. It shouldn't surprise us that the Greek words translated "sound doctrine" in Titus 2:1 (*hygiainousē didaskalia*) literally mean "healthy teaching." When our sermons faithfully exposit the truth of a passage of Scripture, we are giving people nutritious messages that promote spiritual health.

3. More variety in your sermons. Instead of making sermons predictably similar, exposition actually pushes preachers toward greater variety in their sermons. Scottish preacher James Stewart explains why:

> The preacher who expounds his own limited stock of ideas becomes deadly wearisome at last. The preacher who expounds the Bible has endless variety at his disposal. For no two texts say exactly the same thing. Every passage has a quite distinctive meaning. It is not the Holy Spirit's way to repeat Himself.[4]

---

4. James Stewart, *Heralds of God* (New York: Charles Scribner's Sons, 1946), 109.

Those who set their hearts to be expository preachers actually lift a burden off their souls. The decision to faithfully "expose" the message of Scripture in our sermons relieves us of the pressure of devising novel or impressive things to say. It is the Word that speaks with authority and power, the Word that penetrates to the "division of soul and of spirit" (Hebrews 4:12), the Word that feeds hungry hearts, the Word that changes lives.

STAYING ON THE PATH

Choosing to head down the expository path is essential, but it is not enough. After selecting the right homiletical path, we must determine to stay on the path. It's quite possible for a preacher to be mentally committed to expository preaching but functionally engaged in something else.

Duane Litfin, one of my preaching professors at seminary, explains what it means to stay on the expository path. "The substance of your preaching should be both derived from and—here is the kicker—transmitted through the study of a passage of the Bible. This is what it means to say a sermon is expository."[5]

Litfin is on to something important when he calls for sermons "transmitted through the study of a passage." Here is where many preachers wander off the expositional path. The messages they prepare stray far afield from the author's flow of thought. As a result, they wind up in the homiletical weeds.

---

5. Duane Litfin, "New Testament Challenges to Big Idea Preaching," in Keith Willhite and Scott M. Gibson, eds., *The Big Idea of Biblical Preaching* (Grand Rapids: Baker Books, 1998), 55.

Expository sermons, at their best, follow the terrain of the text. The sermon is developed in a way that leads people to track with the biblical author's flow of thought as expressed in the passage. The preacher's explanations, declarations, applications, and gospel invitation all grow out of the soil of the text. At times the passage even provides some of the preacher's illustrations. This is what Litfin means when he speaks of having the "substance" of our sermon being "transmitted through the study of a passage."

In short, expository preachers don't just read the text at the start of the sermon or use the text as a starting point for their own thoughts. The passage is not just the trailhead for the sermon; it is the trail! Expository preachers work hard to keep the minds and hearts of their hearers in close proximity to God's Word.

How do we walk out a commitment to selecting and staying on the expository path as we prepare and preach our sermons? Here are three steps that will lead us in the right direction in sermon exegesis, development, and delivery.

In your sermon exegesis, give primary energy to understanding what the biblical writer said. Through careful exegesis and prayerful reflection, seek to track the author's flow of thought and discover his pastoral purpose. Resist the pull to chart your own homiletical path but seek to faithfully retrace the biblical author's conceptual footsteps.

As you develop your sermons, craft them so they lead people on a journey through the passage, following the biblical author's flow of thought. Make it your goal to help your hearers clearly see how your explanation and applications come right from the passage.

Finally, keep people's attention on the text of Scripture as you deliver your sermon. Don't simply read the passage at the outset of the message and then, figuratively or literally, put your Bible down and make your own way forward. Instead, regularly and repeatedly point people to important features of the text. Heed the wise counsel John Piper offers beginning preachers (which applies equally to seasoned ones!):

> Again and again my advice to beginning preachers is, "Quote the text! Quote the text! Say the actual words of the text again and again. Show the people where your ideas are coming from." Most people do not easily see the connections a preacher sees between his words and the words of the text he is preaching from.[6]

Two roads diverge in the homiletical woods. Along one path walk preachers who *bring* their thoughts to the text, using Scripture to support their own ideas. Along the other path go preachers who *bend* their thoughts to the text, submitting their ideas to Scripture. Only preachers who consistently choose to bend their thoughts to the text walk on the expository path, thus reassuring their hearts by knowing that the power behind their sermons is from God and not their own opinions. For too long this has been the road less traveled. Thankfully, there are promising signs of change. God is raising up a generation

---

6. John Piper, *Preaching and the Supremacy of God* (Grand Rapids: Baker Books, 1990), 88.

of preachers committed to staying on the expository path. I encourage you to be one of them.

If you set your heart to take the expository path, what can you expect to happen? Will expository preaching have an immediate and increased impact on your hearers? Not always, and this brings us to the next way we as preachers can strengthen our souls and guard our hearts: we right-size our expectations.

19
RIGHT-SIZE YOUR EXPECTATIONS

When it comes to the impact your preaching makes in people's lives, how would you describe your expectations? High or low? Realistic or optimistic? Do you anticipate that God's Spirit will work through your message in dramatic ways? In quiet ways? In any way?

Expectations are a tricky thing for us as preachers. On one hand, we know we should have high expectations. After all, the Word of God is living and active, able to penetrate the hardest of hearts and bring about spiritual transformation (Hebrews 4:12). What's more, our God can do "far more abundantly than all we ask or think, according to the power at work within us" (Ephesians 3:20). We've been personally and powerfully impacted by sermons we've heard. We've also seen God graciously use our preaching of the gospel to change someone's eternal destiny. So we have good reason for great expectations.

On the other hand, many of us have preached long enough to know that dramatic changes rarely come from an individual message. Judging by the typical conversations in the lobby immediately after the Sunday service—about ballgames, business, or barbecues—we sometimes wonder if our sermons are having any impact at all. We can also look at the lives of some who have listened to our preaching for years and not see much evidence of significant spiritual progress. Perhaps we should lower our expectations to lessen our frustrations. As Dr. Richard Swenson says, "Unrealistic expectations are premeditated resentments."[1]

Many of us live with some tension when it comes to expectations. We want to preach full of faith but don't want to wind up full of disappointment. We want to aim high but not sink low if we don't see immediate results. So to keep our hearts strong, we will need to right-size our expectations.

When it comes to resetting expectations as a preacher, I've benefitted from reflecting on Jesus' story of the four soils (Luke 8:4–15). This parable helps us calibrate our expectations in a theologically wise way. Jesus' parable reminds us that as we faithfully broadcast God's Word, we can expect (1) different

---

1. Richard Swenson, *In Search of Balance* (Colorado Springs: NavPress, 2010), 174.

kinds of results, (2) incremental rates of growth, and (3) varying amounts of fruit.

DIFFERENT KINDS OF RESULTS

Jesus told the parable of the soils to explain the spectrum of responses to his preaching. He pictured his message as the seed and his hearers as the soil. The determining variable in the different responses to his preaching was the condition of the soil—the condition of the heart and life of the hearer.

The same seed produced different results in the various soils. The seed that fell on the path never penetrated the soil and never germinated. It was immediately stolen away by Satan and quickly forgotten. The seed falling on rocky soil had an immediate but short-lived impact. The seed landing among the thorns showed early promise but proved ultimately unproductive, choked out by the worries and cares of life. Only the seed landing on good soil took root and bore fruit.

Jesus' parable should shape our expectations as preachers. On any given Sunday, all four soils show up at church. As a result, we should anticipate that our sermons will have different effects on those who listen.

Those whose hearts are hard will not get much out of the message, regardless of our faithful preparation and passionate presentation. I once saw a cartoon showing a man sitting in his office at work. The caption read, "Jim remembers something his pastor said in last Sunday's sermon." That sounds encouraging until we learn that Jim remembers his pastor saying, "Is it hot in here, or is it just me? Could someone please check the thermostat?" For those whose hearts have become hardened, this may be about all they remember from last week's sermon.

Thankfully, we also preach to those with honest and good hearts (Luke 8:15). These people receive the word implanted that can save their souls (James 1:21). They prove to be more than hearers of the Word but doers as well (James 1:22). The same message that deflects off the hearts of the hardened gets absorbed and applied in their lives in a fruitful way.

All this implies we should preach with dual expectations. We should realistically expect some to remain unmoved and unchanged by our best efforts at preaching God's Word. At the same time, we should be optimistic, anticipating others will come ready to receive and respond to God's Word in life-shaping ways. Paradoxically, we should preach with both high and low expectations for the impact of our messages.

INCREMENTAL RATES OF GROWTH

The parable of the soils helps us on another level as well. It not only reminds us to expect different kinds of results, it teaches us to expect different rates of growth.

Jesus' agricultural metaphor highlights the truth that growth occurs over time. In fact, incremental, unspectacular growth is the norm. Occasionally, plants spring up in visible ways; typically, growth is far less dramatic. What's true for plants is generally the case for people as well.

Like many parents, Linda and I had a wall in our basement where we charted the physical growth of our kids. Every six months or so, we'd stand them up against the wall and mark their current height. Sometimes growth had been dramatic—an inch in less than a year. Other times, growth had been slower. But almost all of the time, physical growth was difficult to detect on a day-to-day basis. Only our semi-annual measurements revealed the changes that had been taking place over time.

What's true of physical growth is true for spiritual growth: it normally occurs incrementally. While Christians do experience growth spurts, most growth in grace is gradual, difficult to detect on a week-by-week basis. This should encourage us to keep preaching the Word even when we fail to see dramatic evidence of spiritual growth in the lives of our hearers.

I remember a conversation I had with my son Michael when he served as a youth pastor. He'd just heard a radio interview with a youth ministry specialist who advised youth leaders to spend less time preparing messages and more time making personal contact with students. After all, the youth expert argued, students will not remember your messages but will remember you came to their soccer games or took them to Starbucks.

My son, who had been working hard to prepare scriptural messages for the weekly youth group meetings, felt confused and discouraged by what he heard. Should he jettison his efforts to prepare biblical messages for the group? Did his teaching ministry have any value?

I asked him a question: "How many of Mom's meals do you remember from your growing up years?" He remembered only a few—birthday meals, Thanksgiving dinners. I reminded him his mom had made nutritious meals every day for years, even though he had forgotten the specifics of what she served. However, without her faithful work of providing nutritious meals, he would not have grown up healthy and strong.

The same holds true for the spiritual meals preachers prepare. People may only remember a few of our sermons, but faithfully feeding them God's Word helps them grow up to be healthy and strong Christians. Growth may look unspectacular in the short run but it's still significant in the long run.

VARYING AMOUNTS OF FRUIT

There's one more lesson preachers can take from Jesus' parable of the soils: we can expect our preaching to produce different amounts of fruit in the lives of our hearers.

The seed planted in good soil produced a yield of thirty, sixty, or hundredfold. This truth reminds us that, even among those with honest and good hearts, the impact of our messages will not be uniform. We should expect differing amounts of spiritual fruit in the lives of those who respond to the Word. The fact that some show a hundredfold rate of growth should not cause us to dismiss the thirty- or sixtyfold changes in others. As Paul reminded the Corinthians, it is God who "gives the growth" (1 Corinthians 3:7).

All in all, Jesus' parable of the soils prompts us to preach with both raised and realistic expectations. We get a picture of what this looks like in the ministry of Charles Spurgeon. Spurgeon stepped into the pulpit with great expectations that God would use his Word to save the lost and sanctify the saved. Spurgeon expected other preachers to have the same outlook. A pastor once came to Spurgeon for advice, admitting his disappointment that so few trusted Christ for salvation when he preached. Spurgeon reportedly asked the discouraged pastor, "But surely you do not always expect conversions when you preach?" "No, of course I do not," the minister replied. "Well, then," Spurgeon said, "be it unto you according to your faith."[2] A preacher's raised expectations evidence his robust, Christ-honoring faith.

While Spurgeon preached with soaring expectations, he remained theologically grounded and realistic at the same time. As he ascended each step up to his pulpit, he silently whispered, "I believe in the Holy Spirit."[3] He understood that unless the Spirit of God worked through the Word he proclaimed, nothing of eternal significance would happen.

So should you have high or low expectations when it comes to the impact of your preaching? The answer is yes. On one hand, preach with the sober realization that you cannot change a person's heart or bring about spiritual transformation—even with your best sermons. At the same time, preach with the confident assurance that God's Spirit uses his Word to bring about the miracle of new birth and spiritual growth. As you step up

---

2. A. T. Pierson, *From the Pulpit to the Palm-Branch: A Memorial of C. H. Spurgeon* (New York: A. C. Armstrong and Son, 1892), 155.

3. Steven J. Lawson, *The Gospel Focus of Charles Spurgeon* (Sanford, FL: Reformation Trust Publishing, 2012), 106.

to speak, quietly echo Charles Spurgeon's prayer: "I believe in the Holy Spirit."

When we allow Scripture to set and shape our expectations as preachers, we develop a greater sense of security in the confidence that God's Spirit is at work. As we will see in the following chapter, internal security is another important way we can guard our hearts and strengthen our souls to proclaim God's Word.

20
DEVELOP INTERNAL SECURITY

Preachers who believe in *eternal* security can still struggle when it comes to *internal* security. I know from personal experience. While I'm solid in my conviction that God will never let me go, I sometimes get shaky in my confidence as a preacher. As a Christian, I'm secure; as a preacher, I can get insecure.

My insecurities are surfaced by the feedback (or lack of it) I receive when I preach. Feedback tests my sense of significance and security. Over the years, I've seen my internal security rise or fall like the stock market depending on whether comments trend more toward compliments or criticisms.

When you light it up as a preacher, you can feel successful. But you won't necessarily feel secure. That's because preaching well actually raises the bar of people's expectations, adding more pressure to your life. You get the sense you are only as good as your last sermon.

On the other hand, when you struggle as a preacher—when people seem listless or start leaving the church—you can feel like a failure. As critiques start to outweigh kudos, you can develop "Sunday anxiety" and lose your internal security.

SUCH AS IS COMMON TO PREACHERS

Receiving feedback comes with the territory for us as preachers. Invariably, some of it will uplift and some deflate. I take consolation in knowing the apostle Paul faced his share of commendations and critiques as a preacher. If Paul were writing a letter to preachers he could say, "No feedback has overtaken you that is not common to pastors."

If you read Paul's letters, noting his remarks about preaching, you'll discover Paul experienced the sting of criticism. Some who heard him preach openly dismissed his speaking abilities: "For they say, 'His letters are weighty and strong, but his bodily presence is weak, and his speech of no account.'" (2 Corinthians 10:10). Let that last zinger sink in—"his speaking amounts to nothing." Ouch. The very fact Paul could quote this caustic comment shows it stung him and stuck with him. If Paul got panned for his preaching, why should you expect to be exempt from hearing hurtful words?

On the other hand, Paul also received high praise for his preaching. While he certainly had some haters in the church at Corinth, he also had fans. In fact, some folks in Corinth picked him as their favorite preacher (1 Corinthians 1:12). While we may not have a devoted fan club, some in our congregations will express gratitude for our sermons and affirmation of our abilities.

To prepare our hearts for the feedback we will receive as preachers, we need to develop a strong sense of internal security. But just how do we do that? How do we strengthen our souls so we are not overly elevated by praise or thoroughly deflated by criticism? How do we become internally secure as preachers?

STAYING INTERNALLY SECURE

Here again Paul's example helps us. In his final letter to Timothy, Paul blends theology with autobiography to explain his own sense of identity. Consider what Paul wrote in 2 Timothy 1:8–12.

> Therefore do not be ashamed of the testimony about our Lord, nor of me his prisoner, but share in suffering for the gospel by the power of God, who saved us and called us to a holy calling, not because of our works but because of his own purpose and grace, which he gave us in Christ Jesus before the ages began, and which now has been manifested through the appearing of our Savior Christ Jesus, who abolished death and brought life and immortality to light through the gospel, for which I was appointed a preacher and apostle and teacher, which is why I suffer as I do.

Note the flow of Paul's thinking in these verses. He begins by rejoicing in the saving grace of God. Salvation does not result from "anything we have done" but from God's "own purpose and grace" (1:9). This grace was given "in Christ Jesus before the ages began" (1:9) and then revealed "through the appearing of our Savior Christ Jesus" (1:10). Now all who respond to Christ in faith receive "life and immortality" (1:10). That's the good news!

After writing about his salvation in Christ, Paul refers to his calling to preach the gospel, "for which I was appointed a preacher and apostle and teacher" (1:11). Paul had a clear sense of his calling to preach God's truth. This calling to service framed his self-understanding and formed an important part of his identity. But it was not the primary or foundational part of his identity. Remember the order of his words in these verses. He highlighted his salvation calling *before* his service calling. Paul's self-understanding was grounded in his salvation identity (who he was in Christ) before it was based on his service identity (what he did in ministry).

Paul's identity in Christ stabilized his internal security. If we hope to keep our internal security as preachers, we must make sure our sense of identity comes from our salvation rather than our service.

MISPLACED IDENTITY

All this might sound rather basic and obvious to those of us who preach the gospel. Of course our salvation identity comes prior to our service identity. However, ministry has a way of getting us to subtly shift our focus. Without realizing it, we begin to find our primary identity in our ministry service. And as we do, we start to struggle with our internal security. The feedback we receive suddenly looms larger in our thinking. Compliments become overly important to us; critiques become disproportionally devastating. Preaching becomes a way to prove ourselves.

There's a poignant scene in the movie *Chariots of Fire* where Harold Abrahams speaks of the fear that drives him as a sprinter. As he prepares for the 100-meter finals, he tells a teammate: "In one hour's time I will be out there again. I will raise my eyes and look down that corridor, four feet wide, with ten lonely seconds to justify my whole existence. But will I?"

When our primary identity gets wrapped up in our performance as preachers, we start to think like Harold Abrahams. We step up to the platform, raise our eyes and look over the congregation, with thirty lonely minutes to justify our existence—if not to others, at least to ourselves. What a terribly insecure way to live.

But the damage runs deeper than just our own internal sense of security. If we get the order reversed—finding our primary identity in our service for Christ rather than our salvation in Christ—we actually become dangerous in ministry. Instead of preaching to meet the needs of others, we preach to meet our own needs—our insatiable thirst for affirmation and validation. We also become tempted to modify our message to sustain the approval of our audience. In a sense, we become parasitic preachers, living off the very sheep we were called to serve.

INTERNALLY SECURE

Back in my university days, God began to teach me the importance of finding my primary identity in my salvation rather than my service. I had been asked to emcee a large concert on campus. The thought of messing up in front of my peers paralyzed me as I prepared my remarks. A friend stopped by my room and sensed my inner agitation. He wondered why I was so anxious, and I told him about my fears of speaking at the concert. "What would happen if you do a terrible job?" he asked. When I didn't respond, he persisted: "Really, what if things go badly?" Annoyed, I told him I didn't even want to think about that possibility.

He finally left but I couldn't escape his questions. They kept replaying in my head. What would I do if things went south? How would I handle it? In that moment, God's Spirit graciously came to my rescue, giving me an insight that changed my entire perspective. I still remember the sentence that brought clarity and peace to my troubled heart: "I don't serve the Lord so he will love me more; I serve him because he couldn't love me more." In other words, my salvation identity—being loved and saved by God's grace—was to be the motivation for my service identity.

The next night at the concert, I stepped up to speak with a deep sense of peace. This inner security enabled me to do a better job than I would have done if I had remained uptight and tense.

I wish I could say this insight forever freed me from the tendency to find my identity in ministry performance. Honesty compels me to acknowledge the battle for internal security was not won on a single night. I continually must remind myself to find my identity in my salvation rather than my service. As I do, I'm much less apt to be deflated by critical feedback or inflated by commendation.

This side of heaven, I suspect most preachers will struggle when it comes to finding internal security. Like Paul, we will be stung by critical assessments. We will also relish heartfelt affirmations. However, as we find our primary source of identity in our salvation, our inner world will not fluctuate wildly based on the responses we receive. Our growing sense of inner security will both stabilize our souls and enable us to better serve Christ as preachers.

When it comes to feedback about our sermons, preachers who are married have a God-given source for honest, helpful input. That's why, as we will see in the next chapter, to strengthen our souls we must listen to our closest ally.

21

LISTEN TO YOUR CLOSEST ALLY

King Solomon understood that an "excellent wife" was "far more precious than jewels" (Proverbs 31:10). Dietrich Bonhoeffer understood that too—even though he never married. When teaching his seminary students about preaching, he spoke of the priceless value of a wife's sermon smarts: "The pastor has a right to know whether God's word was audible in his sermons. ... The task of the pastor's wife is to perform this service. But the pastor must seek it! ... Thank God if you have a wife who genuinely can criticize you!"[1]

---

1. Dietrich Bonhoeffer, *Theological Education at Finkenwalde: 1935–1937*, ed. Victoria J. Barnett and Barbara Wojhoski, trans. Douglas W. Stott, vol. 14, Dietrich Bonhoeffer Works (Minneapolis: Fortress Press, 2013), 508–9.

Back in my seminary days, Don Sunukjian told us that after we'd served a church for five years, the only one who would be honest with us about our preaching was our wife. Sunukjian was right. After five years, the folks who can't stand your preaching will be long gone. Most of the rest will have adjusted to you, appreciating your strengths and accepting your weaknesses. Not wanting to be hurtful—or thinking it's useless anyway—they won't be able or willing to give a constructive critique of your preaching. That's why a wife who speaks the truth in love (Ephesians 4:15) proves so valuable for strengthening the hearts of those called to preach God's Word.[2]

A WIFE'S PERSPECTIVE

What makes a wife's perspective so valuable? Let me highlight three big reasons.

First, she sees life and hears sermons from a woman's perspective. Your wife brings a viewpoint that reflects many other women, who generally comprise at least half the congregation. Her sensitivities will pick up on things men overlook or dismiss. Seeking her input on your sermons will make your sermons

---

2. Throughout this chapter I refer to the preacher's spouse as his "wife." I realize not all preachers are married. I also affirm the glorious truth that God gifts both men and women to be effective teachers of his Word—I'm married to a woman who is a gifted Bible teacher. My study of Scripture has led me to embrace a complementarian position that maintains God calls godly men to serve as the preaching/teaching elders for Christ's church (1 Timothy 2:11–12; 3:2; 5:17). I recognize sincere Christians have differing convictions on this matter. Since the role of "closest ally" can be filled by a wise, godly friend for unmarried preachers or by an honest, supportive husband for women who preach and teach God's Word, the insights in this chapter can benefit all preachers.

more balanced and believable—especially to the women in your congregation.

Second, she supports you more than anyone else. God gave you your wife as your closest ally. A godly wife possesses what G. K. Chesterton called "a strange and strong loyalty."[3] She wants to see you excel and will defend you when others desert you. Her words of encouragement and affirmation will sustain you when others are silent or critical. If my wife, Linda, senses the sermon was a winner, I rejoice. Her approval is disproportionately important to me; I trust her opinion more than anyone else's.

Third, she can keep you humble like no one else. Having lived with you, she has a realistic view of who you are. She can detect insincerity, hypocrisy, cowardice, pride, or exaggeration in your words better than anyone else (your kids are a close second). If you have nurtured a relationship of love and trust, she will keep you from thinking too highly of yourself.[4]

ASKING FOR INPUT

How can you get the most profit from your wife's honest feedback? Ask for it. I realize this seems rather obvious, but it's often overlooked. If you want your wife to be part of your preaching ministry, invite her in. Tell her you value her views

---

3. G. K. Chesterton, *Orthodoxy* (Glasgow: William Collins Sons & Co., 1908), 70.

4. I realize that Christian wives, like their husbands, are not always "in step with the Spirit" (Galatians 5:25). Their observations and opinions are not infallible. For this reason, Scripture must stand over and above our spouse's critiques or commendations.

and will commit to prayerfully weighing whatever she tells you rather than prematurely dismissing it.

When it comes to asking for your wife's honest feedback, I'd encourage you to ask for it both before and after your sermon. Invite her input before you preach your message. This can take the form of talking through your sermon passage or having her read the draft of your manuscript. Ask her to point out any parts of the message that seem unclear or important aspects of the text you may be missing. Her comments will give you a sense of how the sermon will impact others in the congregation.

Make sure you ask early enough in the week to have time to make any needed changes. Ask her input while the sermonic cement is still wet, before it hardens into its final form. Don't wait until Saturday night—or worse yet, the drive to church on Sunday morning.

Then, invite her input *after* you preach the message. But here's an important qualifier: wait. That's the advice Don Sunukjian gave us in his homiletics course. Sunukjian told us he asked his wife to wait until Thursday before giving him honest feedback on the previous Sunday's sermon. If his wife critiqued him on Sunday or Monday, Sunukjian said he was still too emotionally vulnerable and likely to be overly defensive. By Thursday, he was focused on next Sunday's message; last Sunday's sermon was old news. By Thursday, he was able to hear her comments more dispassionately and respond to them more objectively.

Over the years, my wife and I have put this wise advice into practice. There have been Sundays when Linda was unusually quiet on our drive home. At times, I've probed to see what she was thinking: "How did you sense things went with my sermon today?" Sometimes she has responded by quietly saying, "I'm waiting until Thursday."

When it comes to benefiting from your wife's input on your preaching, one crucial factor will determine whether or not you benefit from her insights: you have to be willing to receive her comments without pouting or punishing. Being defensive or becoming offensive when she has words of critique will shut down the process in short order. Most wives are smart enough to discern when we are asking for evaluation but only want affirmation. So we must learn to silence our inner lawyer and absorb her words even if we don't initially agree with her analysis.

Over the years, my wife has been my most consistent source of affirmation as a preacher. She's also served as my most astute critic. For example, she has pointed out times when I did not adequately or accurately bring out a rebuke or warning from a passage I was preaching. She has voiced her concern that I can underemphasize biblical exhortations, letting people off too easy. While this critique has stung, it has been easier to accept coming from my most supportive listener. It's also been echoed by some trusted colleagues who observed the same tendency in me. Listening carefully to her perceptions has helped me grow into a better preacher.

NOT LAYING EGGS

A married preacher who won't listen to his wife's compliments and critiques will be poorer for it. If you don't listen to the feedback your wife whispers in private, you may eventually hear it spoken publicly from the rooftops. On the other hand, if you leverage the wisdom and insights of your wife, you and your congregation will be richer for it.

My favorite preacher story is about a pastor who discovered a shoebox underneath his bed. On the box his wife had written, "Please do not open." Overcome with curiosity, he opened it anyway. Inside he found four eggs and multiple stacks of twenty-dollar bills. That night at dinner he confessed he'd found and opened the box. He could see she was disappointed and a bit embarrassed. So he asked her to explain. She replied, "Over the years, whenever you've preached a poor sermon—laid an egg—I put an egg in the box." The pastor breathed a sigh of relief. "Well," he said, "I've been preaching for thirty-five years. Four eggs isn't too bad!" Then he asked, "But what was with all the money?" "Oh," she answered, "whenever I got a dozen eggs I sold them."

Preachers who listen to the honest input of their wives on Thursdays are much less likely to lay eggs on Sundays.

If what we hear on Thursdays can help us get ready for Sundays, so can what we do on Saturday nights. Making the most of Saturday night is another way we strengthen our souls to proclaim God's Word.

22

MAKE THE MOST OF SATURDAY NIGHTS

Preachers have something in common with NFL football players. For both of us, Sunday is Game Day. While it's true we hit the field all week long, in a special sense, Game Day arrives each Sunday.

For years, I've said Game Day for me as a preacher starts on Saturday night. To be in the best shape possible on Sunday morning, I've got to make good use of Saturday night—not primarily for sermon preparation, but soul preparation. Making the most of Saturday nights is one of the ways preachers can strengthen their souls to proclaim God's Word.

For many years, my wife, Linda, and I have chosen to keep Saturday nights as preparation time for Sundays. We rarely accept invitations out on Saturday evenings (rarely, not never). We thank people for the invitation and ask if we can find another time. We've found most people in the congregation understand the idea that we spend Saturday evening getting spiritually and physically ready for Sunday.

The idea of keeping Saturday evenings free was something Dietrich Bonhoeffer taught his students at the seminary he started in Finkenwalde, Germany: "By all means keep Saturday evening free. ... Refuse basically all invitations within the congregation."[1] Bonhoeffer knew spending time with a few folks on Saturday evenings could result in shortchanging many more on Sunday mornings.

THREE WAYS TO MAKE THE MOST OF SATURDAY NIGHTS

I recognize the fine line between pastoral wisdom and legalism in this matter. Some pastors will counter that being with godly friends on Saturday actually prepares their hearts and minds for Sunday's sermon. If that's the case for you, enjoy the freedom you have in Christ Jesus.

For me, reserving Saturday nights for sermon and soul preparation has proven to be a great help in getting ready for Sundays.

---

1. Dietrich Bonhoeffer, *Theological Education at Finkenwalde: 1935–1937*, ed. Victoria J. Barnett and Barbara Wojhoski, trans. Douglas W. Stott, vol. 14, Dietrich Bonhoeffer Works (Minneapolis: Fortress Press, 2013), 488.

Let me highlight three of my Saturday evening practices and their benefits.

Internalization. In my normal pastoral rhythm, I finish preparing my sermon manuscript by Thursday or Friday. So Saturday is not normally a time for sermon preparation. Instead, it's a time for sermon internalization.

As I confess in chapter 8, I came out of seminary with the intention of memorizing my manuscript. After my wife's honest feedback, I shifted my focus to internalizing my messages. Internalizing, for me, means getting clear on the message flow—so clear that I can walk through the message, confidently knowing what comes next.

Saturday nights give me time to finish internalizing the message. I sit with my manuscript and go through it several times, circling key words, writing prompts in the margins, and changing words or sentences that feel awkward or unclear.

Like a pitcher rubbing up a new baseball before throwing it, I work my manuscript over before I'm ready to preach it. The process of marking up my manuscript several times helps me internalize both the overall flow of the sermon and key concepts I want to communicate the next day.

Intercession. As I mentioned in chapter 17, preachers would be wise to pray throughout the process of sermon preparation. While prayer for our sermons should not be limited to the night before we preach, I've found Saturday evenings a wonderful time for extended prayer for the impact of the Sunday message.

Early in our marriage, Linda and I began a practice of praying together on Saturday nights for the ministry we anticipated on Sunday. After the kids were in bed, we would kneel by our couch and ask God to work powerfully in the lives of the people of our congregation. Now that our kids are grown and gone, we still regularly follow the same pattern. We pray for our own hearts. We pray for the impact of Sunday's sermon. We pray about the hallway conversations we will have before and after the service. We pray for spiritual protection, remembering Jesus taught us to ask the Father to "keep us from the evil one" (Matthew 6:13). We also pray for other pastors and churches in our community and across the country.

By the way, we've discovered that most of our marital tensions somehow surface on Saturdays. There's been too much of a pattern here to conclude this is simply a matter of chance. We're convinced our spiritual adversary chooses that time to exacerbate the normal tension points that can get us sideways with one another. The devil knows strife on Saturday can sabotage Sunday. This is another reason why praying together on Saturday evenings is vital to our ministry as a couple. It helps us move into Sunday in a good place with one another.

Interlude. Saturday evenings can provide preachers with an interlude—a space of time between events. Pastors often come into Sunday morning having lived at a relentless pace throughout the week. Ministry and family fill our days to the brim—and beyond it. Sundays bring a burst of activity as well.

Saturday nights can provide an opportunity to rest between a full week and the flurry on Sunday. So in addition to taking time to internalize my sermon and intercede for the message, I have found it life-giving to take some time to relax on Saturday evening. We also try to deal with Sunday logistics on Saturdays to take some of the stress out of getting out the door on time for church. Then I also head to bed early enough to get a good night of sleep.

Over the years, I've learned if I go full speed all day Saturday, falling into bed late and then rising early on Sunday morning, I am tired and depleted by the time I step up to preach. Without some downtime on Saturday evening, I've found it harder to be up for Sunday morning. Since I want to give it my best, I try to be at my best.

SATURDAY IN THE PARK

I don't want to give the impression that Saturdays are only about sermon and soul preparation. While this has been true for most of my Saturday nights, it's not been the case for Saturday mornings and afternoons. Those have been reserved for family time or home upkeep. For many years, I used my minimal culinary skills to make Saturday breakfast—usually pancakes or French toast. After breakfast, each Saturday had its own schedule. Mowing lawns, running errands, kids' sports—you name it. Occasionally there were ministry events, but generally I focused on the family.

My wife would tell you I tended to be emotionally and physically present with the family until sometime in the late afternoon.

Then she could tell I began to move into Sunday mode. After dinner, Game Day preparation started in earnest.

To make this rhythm a reality, I have had to have my sermon finished by Friday. This deadline has proven a good discipline. Since work (even sermon preparation) tends to fill available time, having a self-imposed deadline to finish my message by Friday has helped me work more efficiently during the week.

CALLING THE AUDIBLES

For some of you, the specifics of what I'm proposing won't work. Pastors with Saturday night services, for example, will have to find a preparation rhythm that works for their schedules. For a brief time, a church I pastored experimented with a Saturday evening service. When we did, my Saturday family time became limited to morning hours. After lunch, I went into preparation mode.

Even if the rhythm I've described does work most of the time, there will be exceptions. Over the years, there certainly have been Saturday evenings when we've not stayed home and followed our normal pattern. Sometimes it was a dinner engagement that couldn't easily be moved to another day. Sometimes it was a concert or special ministry event. On those nights, I tried to carve out time in the afternoon to do what I usually did in the evening hours. I also trusted God's grace to still empower me on Sunday. I even wrote some of this chapter on a Saturday that didn't cooperate with my carefully planned system for Saturdays! Linda and I got a call from a family member who was going through a very traumatic time. So rather than having a quiet, peaceful evening, we were on the phone getting more information and trying to decide how to help carry the load. Life goes that way.

Thankfully, we serve a God who shows his power and grace in these very kinds of situations. He can help us deal with the unexpected on Saturday nights and still give us strength to preach his Word on Sundays. So while I still recommend keeping a regular rhythm of reserving Saturday evenings for internalization, intercession, and an interlude of rest, I am mindful that our trust is not in our careful plans or preparation but in God's goodness and grace.

So far, I've advocated a number of spiritual practices that can strengthen a pastor's soul. I trust that, in most cases, the connection between my counsel and the goal of guarding and keeping our hearts has been rather apparent. That may not be the case with what comes next. In the following chapter, I highlight a way to strengthen your soul as a preacher that may seem surprising: doing the work of an evangelist.

23
DO THE WORK
OF AN EVANGELIST

Have you noticed that, in the same passage where Paul calls Timothy to "preach the word," he also tells him to be engaged in evangelism? "As for you, always be sober-minded, endure suffering, do the work of an evangelist, fulfill your ministry" (2 Timothy 4:5). Not all pastors and teachers have an evangelist's gifts; however, God expects us to take part in an evangelist's work.

Preachers know Jesus called all his disciples to make disciples by being his witnesses. You may have preached your share of sermons from Matthew 28:18–20 or Acts 1:8. So when we hear Paul's call to Timothy to do the work of an evangelist, we are theologically in agreement. Unfortunately, many of us are functionally out of agreement. While we love the gospel, apart from Sunday sermons, we rarely speak the gospel to someone who needs Christ.

Ask yourself: When did I last have a gospel conversation with a friend, neighbor, or acquaintance who is "separated from Christ … having no hope and without God in the world" (Ephesians 2:12)? Paul's charge to Timothy about doing the work of an evangelist carries a clear implication for us as preachers: we can't fulfill our ministries if we aren't active in evangelism.

WHY IT'S DIFFICULT
AND WHY IT MATTERS

I know that doing the work of an evangelist presents some unique challenges for pastors. After all, we spend most of our waking hours caring for Christians: preparing sermons, planning and problem solving, counseling, and discipling. Besides all we do for the church, we also provide care for our own families, "for if someone does not know how to manage his own household, how will he care for God's church?" (1 Timothy 3:5–6).

When Paul wrote to Timothy, though, he certainly realized Timothy felt stretched by his pastoral responsibilities. He understood Timothy's tender temperament and physical challenges ("your stomach and your frequent ailments," 1 Timothy 5:23). He also knew proclaiming the gospel could bring suffering or even land Timothy in prison, like it had done for Paul (2 Timothy 1:8). But Paul also knew evangelism was an integral part of Timothy's calling as a preacher. That's why he doesn't give Timothy a pass when it comes to doing the work of an evangelist. And that's why we don't get a pass either.

On the most foundational level, the reason pastors need to be engaged in evangelism is obvious—Jesus gave his Great Commission to all his followers (Matthew 28:18–20). That includes pastors. But I'm convinced there is a specific, strategic reason why God wants pastors and teachers to do the work of an evangelist: He wants those who preach his Word to the church to share his heart for the world. He wants preachers to demonstrate a heart for the gospel in order to set an example for the congregation and shape the culture of the church.

God designed his world so we reproduce after our own kind. That's true both physically and spiritually. As Jesus explained, "A disciple is not above his teacher, but everyone when he is fully trained will be like his teacher" (Luke 6:40). Congregations become like their leaders—for better or worse. If a pastor only preaches about evangelism without being personally engaged in it, people will conclude that giving out the gospel is optional. It's something we affirm on Sunday but avoid on Monday.

On the other hand, when pastors engage in the joys and frustrations of bringing the gospel to their friends and family, the church takes notice. As leaders demonstrate an ongoing, personal commitment to evangelism, a change begins to take place in the congregation. Others catch the excitement. Gospel conversations become a regular part of people's lives throughout the week. In time, the culture of the church begins to shift to be more gospel-focused.

While we may hesitate to make time for evangelism in light of all our other responsibilities, the truth is that when pastors engage in personal evangelism, their example has a positive impact on the life of the congregation. Churches with pastors like this trend toward health and growth. This was the finding of a major survey conducted by LifeWay Research in 2017. The study involved 1,500 phone calls to lead pastors serving evangelical congregations of under two hundred people. The results revealed a significant correlation between the pastor's personal engagement in evangelism and the congregation's growth by conversion. For example, among Southern Baptist churches, the top 20 percent of growing churches had pastors who were more active in doing the work of an evangelist than pastors in the lowest 50 percent of churches. The believers in these congregations became more consistent in praying for unsaved friends, more purposeful in spending time with non-churched people, and more intentional in sharing the gospel and inviting a response.[1] In presenting the survey results to pastoral leaders, Ed Stetzer drives home a key takeaway: "Pastor, no one in your church will share the gospel more than you."[2]

GETTING TO WORK

So where do we find the time and relational energy needed to meaningfully connect with people who need Christ? I can name at least two places.

1. Ed Stetzer and Jeffrey Farmer, "Evangelism in Small Church America: Exclusive Research," July 9, 2017, https://outreachmagazine.com/features/23350-small-church-evangelism.html.

2. Stetzer and Farmer, "Evangelism in Small Church America."

In our sermons. As noted above, Paul's directive to Timothy about evangelism comes in the context of his call to preach God's Word (2 Timothy 4:1–2). The juxtaposition of preaching and evangelism implies that pastors can do the work of an evangelist as they preach the Word. In the preceding passage, Paul had reminded Timothy how he came to saving faith in Christ through hearing the Scriptures from his mother and grandmother: "how from childhood you have been acquainted with the sacred writings, which are able to make you wise for salvation through faith in Christ Jesus" (2 Timothy 3:15). As Paul explained to the Christians in Rome, "So faith comes from hearing, and hearing through the word of Christ" (Romans 10:17).

Faithful exposition of Scripture, including the Old Testament, can have a powerful evangelistic impact. That's one reason our homiletics courses at Heritage Seminary train students to make a "gospel move" in every sermon, beginning from the passage being preached. Charles Spurgeon recounts an older minister's words to a young preacher: "Do you not know that from every little town and village and tiny hamlet in England there is a road leading to London? Whenever I get hold of a text, I say to myself, 'There is a road from here to Jesus Christ, and I mean to keep on his track till I get to him.'"[3] Every biblical text fits into the larger narrative, which centers around and culminates in Christ. As such, every passage provides a trailhead to Christ and his gospel. While the preacher's gospel move may be more extensive in some sermons than

---

3. Charles Spurgeon, *The Soul Winner: How to Lead Sinners to the Saviour* (New York: Fleming H. Revell, 1895), 99.

others, every sermon should point people to Christ and his redemptive work.[4]

When preachers consistently present the gospel message in their expository messages, several positive results often follow. Some who are only "churched" become saved as they see their need for Christ and personally embrace the gospel message. Also, committed believers gain confidence to invite friends to the service knowing that, on any given Sunday, the gospel will be presented in the message.

In our personal witness. Doing the work of an evangelist involves more than preaching the gospel to those who show up for church services. Following the lead of the Good Shepherd, pastors must go after the lost sheep who won't be coming to church anytime soon (Luke 15:4).

How this looks in practice will differ for every pastor based on life stage, gifts, and circumstances. But here's where a preacher's pastoral gifts and skills can shine. Pastors know how to make conversation with strangers, connect people together, and foster a sense of community. When pastors apply their shepherding skills in their neighborhoods and communities, good things happen evangelistically.

Over the years, I've partnered with my wife, Linda, to develop relationships with neighbors and people we've met through

---

4. For more on gospel moves see chapter 9, "Retreating." For help in making a gospel move, see Gary Millar and Phil Campbell, *Saving Eutychus*, chapter 5.

our kids' schools. We've found taking a little relational initiative goes a long way in building friendships. In each place we've lived, we became the self-appointed "community connection directors." We gathered people for neighborhood barbecues and progressive dinners, Christmas open houses, as well as discussion and dessert nights (on topics such as, "Why is there so much suffering if God is good?"). Out of these gatherings, friendships developed, providing us opportunities to present the gospel or invite friends to an Alpha class, an outreach event at church, or a Sunday service. We've had the joy of seeing God bring people we love to know the Savior who loves them. This kind of joy in the pastor's life becomes contagious in the congregation!

STRENGTHENING YOUR SOUL THROUGH EVANGELISM

Taking the time and making the effort to "do the work of an evangelist" does good things to strengthen our souls and keep our hearts as preachers. It grows our compassion for people who need Christ. It guards us from the hypocrisy that comes from preaching about evangelism but failing to practice what we preach. It also gives us credibility to call others to join in sharing the good news of the gospel.

If a local church is to be dynamically engaged in God's mission of rescuing and redeeming men, women, boys, and girls, the local church's pastor must lead the way. Missional churches are led by pastors who preach the Word and do the work of an evangelist.

If this chapter on evangelism seemed a rather surprising inclusion in a book on strengthening a preacher's soul, what comes next may prove even more unexpected. I'm convinced that guarding our hearts requires guarding our health. We must make sure we don't "kill the horse."

24
DON'T KILL THE HORSE

"God gave me a message to deliver and a horse to ride. Alas, I've killed the horse and now I cannot deliver the message."[1]

Robert Murray M'Cheyne penned these words shortly before he died at the age of twenty-nine. M'Cheyne was an incredibly gifted young preacher, leading a large congregation by age twenty-three. Sadly, he pushed his body until his health broke under the strain of ministry. He killed the horse and could no longer deliver the message.

---

1. "Killed the Horse," Bible.org, February 2, 2009, https://bible.org/illustration/killed-horse.

The seminary professor who told me M'Cheyne's story also quoted a pointed, practical observation made by Dr. Lewis Sperry Chafer, founder of Dallas Seminary: "No one can have a spiritual ministry without a physical body."[2] I know that sounds obvious. Apparently, many of us pastors are oblivious to the obvious. Caring for our souls requires caring for our bodies.[3]

IN THE FOOTSTEPS OF PAUL

As we read Paul's words to Timothy, his pastoral protégé, we rightly focus on our need for spiritual exercise: "Rather train yourself for godliness; for while bodily training is of some value, godliness is of value in every way, as it holds promise for the present life and also for the life to come" (1 Timothy 4:7–8). We tend to overlook the fact that Paul acknowledges the value of "bodily training," which serves us well in "the present life."

Paul and Timothy's lives were far less sedentary than the average pastor in our day. For one thing, they walked to work—and everywhere else! I've read estimates that Paul walked at least 10,000 miles in his lifetime. That's easily more miles than you'd rack up walking round trip across North America from coast to coast. When Paul tells Timothy, "Do your best to come to me soon" (2 Timothy 4:9), he's asking Timothy to make a 1,200-mile trip—much of it on foot. Pastors in Paul's day, along with

---

2. Class lecture by Dr. Bill Lawrence, Dallas Theological Seminary, 1984.

3. As Dan Block points out in his excellent commentary on Ezekiel, the Hebrew word for soul (*nepeš*) often is used to refer to the whole person, including the body. So our understanding of what it means to strengthen our souls must include caring for the physical aspect of our beings. See Block, *The Book of Ezekiel, Chapters 1–24* (Grand Rapids: Eerdmans, 1997), 562.

everyone else, could hardly avoid getting some physical exercise. We have the opposite problem.

BROADUS ON EXERCISE

John Broadus (1827–1925) served as the first homiletics professor at Southern Baptist Theological Seminary. His book *On the Preparation and Delivery of Sermons* was the standard preaching textbook used in seminary classrooms for decades. By all accounts, Broadus was an exceptional expositor. He had a message to deliver. Trouble was, he began killing his horse. Early on in his teaching ministry at Southern, he struggled with chronic health issues, forcing him out of the classroom for extended seasons.

Thankfully, unlike M'Cheyne, he determined to make changes in the way he lived. He began to exercise regularly. Even when ministry became demanding and time consuming, he consistently carved out time for physical exercise. His strength and stamina increased; his sick days decreased.

Broadus became a strong proponent of physical exercise at Southern. He exhorted the preachers he trained to take up some form of physical training. "We must all learn to take ample muscular exercise every day, and a little walking or driving is not enough."[4] He called students to make exercise a top priority in daily life: "Better face a class very imperfectly prepared

---

4. Adam Winters, "Exercise, Preacher: Exhortation from John Broadus," *Towers* 14:2 (September 2015), http://equip.sbts.edu/publications/towers/exercise-preacher-exhortations-from-john-broadus/.

than violate the laws of health."[5] He spoke from personal experience when he said, "I have kept alive, amid many infirmities, and I know it has been through persistent exercise and plenty of sleep."[6]

Broadus warned his students against killing the horse God gave them to ride in life and ministry. He reminded them of Alexander Hodge, brother of Charles Hodge and a uniquely gifted professor at old Princeton: "This admirable man presumed on his always vigorous health, and devoted himself to incessant reading and writing, with an almost total neglect of exercise; and so, at the age of fifty, there came a sudden collapse, and the world lost all those other noble works which he might have been expected to produce."[7]

STEPS TOWARD CHANGE

Preaching, like pastoring in general, will allow us to have a sedentary lifestyle unless we take steps (literally and figuratively) to become more physically active. Thankfully, almost all of us can make the lifestyle changes we need to make for the sake of the message we have to deliver.

Several years ago, Linda and I stayed in a cottage owned by the family of Robert Boyd Munger. You may remember him as the pastor who wrote the well-known booklet *My Heart, Christ's Home*. In the cottage I found another book Munger

5. Winters, "Exercise, Preacher."
6. Winters, "Exercise, Preacher."
7. Winters, "Exercise, Preacher."

had written—near the end of his life—entitled *Leading from the Heart*.[8] In it he tells how he had a midlife health crisis that landed him in the hospital and put him out of ministry for a season. As part of his recovery, he began a practice of daily walks, something he continued "religiously" for the rest of his life. God graciously allowed him to live and continue in ministry many more years. His family is convinced his midlife lifestyle changes helped prolong his life.

I read Munger's book just after being diagnosed with cancer. One of the good results of the cancer experience was the impetus to make some changes in both my diet and exercise. I took the advice of a nutritionist who counseled: "Sell your salad bowl and buy a salad bucket." Along with eating more whole foods and less processed, sugary ones, I strengthened my commitment to consistent exercise.

Dr. Mike Evans, a physician who has taught medicine at both the University of Toronto and at Stanford, has recorded some life-giving words for people who spend an inordinate amount of time sitting—like pastors. In a nine-minute lecture, he advises walking briskly for at least thirty minutes a day.[9]

The health benefits of a thirty-minute walk are surprising; numerous studies show walking ameliorates a host of maladies including anxiety, depression, fatigue, high blood pressure, and diabetes. Dr. Evans cites a fascinating study on the

---

8. Robert B. Munger, *Leading from the Heart: Lifetime Reflections on Spiritual Development* (Downers Grove, IL: InterVarsity Press, 1995).

9. Mike Evans, "23 and ½ Hours: What Is the Single Best Thing We Can Do for Our Health?" December 2, 2011, www.youtube.com/watch?v=aUaInS6HIGo.

benefits of walking conducted by a large gas company in Japan. They discovered employees whose walk to work was under ten minutes showed no positive health differences compared with those who commuted by car or train. However, workers whose daily walk was between eleven and twenty minutes showed a 12 percent decrease in high blood pressure. When the walk was over twenty minutes, high blood pressure rates decreased by 29 percent.

Dr. Evans wraps up his lecture by quoting the ancient doctor Hippocrates, who said, "Walking is man's best medicine." Then he asks a simple, convicting question: "Can you limit your sitting and sleeping to just 23 and ½ hours a day?"[10]

ENOCH WALKS

I realize some pastors reading this have already committed themselves to regular and rigorous workouts: running, biking, lifting, hockey, tennis, swimming. For these pastors, thirty minutes of walking doesn't even qualify as light exercise. However, for many pastors, starting to walk thirty minutes a day would be a big stretch.

If you struggle to limit your sitting and sleeping to just 23 ½ hours a day, I'd challenge you to begin taking "Enoch walks." That's what I call my thirty-minute walks. I took the name "Enoch walks" from Genesis 5:24: "Enoch walked with God." Admittedly, Moses wasn't saying Enoch took thirty-minute walks to improve physical health. However, I use the phrase to remind

---

10. Evans, "23 and ½ Hours."

me that when I go for a thirty-minute walk (outdoors in good weather; on a treadmill in winter), I want to use the time to promote both physical and spiritual health.

So as I walk, I pray. Or listen to music that prompts my soul to offer praise to God. Having my mind and heart active makes the time fly by, even when I'm on the treadmill. Most days, I look forward to getting out of the office and heading out for a thirty-minute prayer walk. Even on days when I go reluctantly, I'm always glad I went. These walks with God have become a non-legalistic, non-negotiable part of my weekly schedule. I don't feel guilty if I miss a day, but making time for an Enoch walk has become a settled priority.

All of us who are preachers have a message to deliver. Each of us has also been given a horse to ride. We must remember that if we fail to care for the horse, we won't be able to carry out our calling and deliver God's message.

When it comes to strengthening your heart as a preacher, each idea I've presented so far has proven helpful to me over the years. But I've saved the best for last. In the final chapter, I get to the heart of what it will take to keep your heart both soft and strong as you proclaim God's Word. That involves keeping your first love.

25
KEEP YOUR FIRST LOVE

The place goes by the name of Mensa Christi, which means "Table of Christ." Situated on the northern shore of the Sea of Galilee, this quiet, rocky beach commemorates the spot Jesus served breakfast to seven of his disciples on a morning after his resurrection.

Of all the places we visited on our trip to Israel, Mensa Christi stands out as one of my favorites. Our group of ministry leaders and spouses gathered in a small, outdoor amphitheater near the shoreline. One pastor read the text of John 21 as we envisioned the disciples sitting round an open fire, eating a breakfast of fish and bread. It wasn't hard to imagine the conversation between Jesus and Peter: "Simon, son of John, do you love me?" "Lord, you know everything; you know that I love you." "Feed my sheep."

Tears fell freely as I reflected on God's grace to a disciple who had recently stumbled badly. John 21 rarely fails to move me. Maybe it's because I identify with Peter. I, too, have made big promises to God and failed to carry them out. I, too, have wondered whether I was really cut out for ministry. There have been times I considered taking up a different line of work—though, in my case, fishing never made the short list of possible options.

But it's not just that I identify with Peter in his stumbling. I also share his deep love for Jesus. Peter's words find an echo in my heart: "Lord, you know all things; you know that I love you. Even when my actions haven't shown it, even when I've failed you and others, you know my heart and know I love you. Often poorly, but truly."

I'm also amazed by the way Jesus recommissions Peter into service, even on the far side of his defection and desertion. "Feed my lambs." "Tend my sheep." "Feed my sheep." Jesus had already called Peter to be a fisher of men (Matthew 4:19). Now he calls him to be a shepherd of sheep.

FEEDING BECAUSE OF LOVE

Many years ago, I heard a seasoned pastor speak about what motivated him to keep going in ministry. He referenced John 21 and Jesus' call to Peter. He explained that earlier in his life, he had heard Christ's commission to feed his sheep. That sense of calling kept him preaching and pastoring—feeding and leading God's people. Pastoral ministry was an expression of his love for Christ and faithfulness to his call.

I, too, have been commissioned to feed Christ's sheep. I'm painfully aware of my own failings; nevertheless, I know I have been called to feed and lead Christ's people as an expression of my love for him.

When it comes to motivations for preaching, we sometimes miss this most basic of all motivators: love for Jesus. Did you notice Jesus didn't ask, "Peter, do you love my *sheep*?" Instead, he only asked, "Do you love *me*?" If our primary motivation for preaching is a love for people, we will struggle when people are hard to love. After all, sheep can wander; sheep can bite. But when ministry motivation arises from a genuine love for Christ, we have good reason to stay faithful— especially since the One who calls us knows our less-than-rock-solid track record. Having been forgiven much by Christ, we love him much and show our love through feeding his sheep as we preach his Word. Like Peter, we willingly embrace the call to "shepherd the flock of God" (1 Peter 5:2). While there are many worthy motivations for ministry, the greatest of these is love. Love for Christ strengthens our souls to faithfully feed Christ's sheep.

FOLLOWING BECAUSE OF LOVE

John 21 doesn't end with Peter's recommissioning to service. The shoreline conversation between Jesus and Peter continues with some news Peter must have found unsettling.

"Truly, truly, I say to you, when you were young, you used to dress yourself and walk wherever you wanted, but when you are old, you will stretch out your hands and another will dress you and carry you where you do not want to go" (21:18). Jesus' words, while cryptic, have an ominous feel. Immediately after welcoming Peter back into ministry, Jesus warns him about his eventual suffering and death.

Understandably, Peter has questions. Wouldn't you? Peter wonders when all this will happen. What will it look like? Will he be able to handle it, or would he crumble again as he had in the high priest's courtyard? As questions must have multiplied in his mind, Peter turns and sees John standing nearby. He asks Jesus whether John is headed for the same kind of painful ending: "Lord, what about this man?" (21:21). Jesus won't go there. "If it is my will that he remain until I come, what is that to you? You follow me!" (21:22). Evidently, John's story is none of Peter's business. All he needs to know is that he is to follow Jesus, wherever it leads and whatever it costs.

In C. S. Lewis's book *The Horse and His Boy*, young Shasta has an encounter with Aslan, not at daybreak on a quiet shoreline, but in the dark of night in a dense forest. Shasta pours out his life story, recounting the painful hardships he has experienced. To his surprise, he learns Aslan had been powerfully present in each of them. Still confused, Shasta asks about Aslan's dealings with Aravis, a young girl he had met on his journeys. "Child," Aslan replies, "I am telling you your story, not hers. I tell no one any story but his own."[1]

---

1. C. S. Lewis, *The Horse and His Boy* (New York: Macmillan, 1954), 141.

Like Peter or Shasta, we sometimes have questions about those around us. We look over our shoulders in ministry and see someone who seems to have it better or at least easier than we do. "Lord, what about this man?" we ask. "Will he experience the kind of hardships I am facing?" But Jesus won't go there. He doesn't tell us another's story. He simply calls us to follow him.

There's a phrase in the text of John 21 that is strangely reassuring to me. After Jesus gives Peter a glimpse of his future, John adds, "This he said to show by what kind of death he was to glorify God" (21:19). I see a promise embedded in these words. Peter's death was not to be viewed as a tragic end to a life of service but as his final act of earthly service, as the God-glorifying finale to his life's song. Jesus viewed his own death through the lens of bringing glory to God. On the night he was arrested he prayed, "Father, the hour has come; glorify your Son that the Son may glorify you" (John 17:1). Peter's death would follow the pattern of his Lord and bring glory to God.

Tradition tells us Peter was crucified like Christ. Jesus' words in John 21:18 are eerily precise: Peter literally did "stretch out his hands." There is some historical evidence that Peter had one final request of those who crucified him: he asked to be crucified upside down, not feeling worthy to die in the same position as his Lord. Peter's love for Jesus strengthened him to follow faithfully to the very end. Love for Christ strengthens our souls to faithfully follow him for a lifetime.

MY JESUS I LOVE THEE

At our daughter's graduation ceremony at Gordon College in the spring of 2008, Judson Carlberg gave the commencement address. Jud had recently retired after serving as the president of the school for the past twenty years. Shortly after announcing his retirement, he was diagnosed with an advanced, aggressive form of cancer. As he addressed these newly minted graduates, all primed to take on life, he spoke to them from John 21. He talked of the grace of God that had come to him in the midst of his suffering, deepening his faith and his love for Christ. He challenged the graduates to follow Jesus for the rest of their lives—no matter where he leads or how their story ends.

At times, I get anxious about how my story will end. Having had cancer once, I sometimes fear it will return. New pains bring new worries. I wonder if there will be a return visit to the oncologist, if cancer will take me to a place I don't want to go again. I don't know the answer to those questions any more than Peter did on the morning of his lakeshore conversation. All I know is that I have been called into Christ's service by his grace. I've been commissioned to feed his people—young and old.

If you are called to preach God's Word, the same holds true for you. So give yourself to the joyful task of studying his Word and preparing sermons, seeking to make them as nourishing and appetizing as possible. Refuse to be paralyzed by the fear of what could happen in the future, focusing instead on what needs to happen in the present. Out of love for the One who has forgiven you and given you this calling, stay faithful until your earthly story ends.

We finished our visit to Mensa Christi inside a small chapel near the water's edge. Our group of pastoral couples crowded inside the stone walls, sparrows darting around above our heads. With a renewed sense of our own calling into ministry, we joined voices to sing a particularly appropriate hymn:

> My Jesus, I love Thee, I know Thou art mine.
>> For Thee all the follies of sin I resign.
> My gracious Redeemer, my Savior art Thou.
>> If ever I loved Thee, my Jesus, 'tis now.[2]

I left Mensa Christi with a renewed sense of calling to ministry. For me, this calling centers on preaching God's Word to feed Christ's people. I also left Mensa Christi with something else, something even more valuable—a renewed sense of love for the One who called me into ministry. Ultimately, keeping our love strong for Christ is the main way we keep our hearts strong as preachers.

---

2. William R. Featherston, "My Jesus I Love Thee," 1864, http://library .timelesstruths.org/music/My_Jesus_I_Love_Thee/.

CONCLUSION

On a bookcase in my office sits a small plaque my seminary preaching professor, Dr. Bill Lawrence, gave me when I graduated. It simply reads, "The Man is the Message."

I'm quite confident Dr. Lawrence, who placed great emphasis on accurate exegesis, realized the wording on the plaque was not strictly true. He knew the message we preach always outsizes and outlasts the man or woman who proclaims it. He had read Isaiah 40: "All flesh is grass, and all its beauty is like the flower of the field. ... The grass withers, the flower fades, but the word of our God will stand forever" (Isaiah 40:6, 8).

The reason he gave me the plaque, and the reason I still display it in my office, is that it highlights an important truth I must never forget: when it comes to preaching, the message and messenger are always closely linked. What we say as preachers cannot be separated from who we are. In this sense, Dr. Lawrence's plaque is right: the man is the message. Or to put it another way: at the heart of preaching is the preacher's heart.

That's why we must follow the admonition given in Proverbs 4:23: "Keep your heart with all vigilance, for from it flow the springs of life." While this instruction applies to all people, it has special implications for preachers. As Jesus reminded the religious teachers of his day, "from the abundance of the heart the mouth speaks" (Matthew 12:34). If the springs of our heart become muddied, the words that flow from our lips will be too.

Keeping our hearts with vigilance will require continual attention and conscious effort. We will need to practice personal soul care, developing a devotional life larger than our sermon preparation. We will need to avoid whatever sullies our souls and repent quickly when sinful thoughts, attitudes, or actions muddy our hearts. Keeping our hearts with vigilance will prompt us to preach the gospel to ourselves every day, reminding ourselves of the saving and sanctifying grace that comes to us in Christ. We must learn to find our identity in our position in Christ, not our performance as preachers. We also keep our hearts by entrusting them to allies who love us enough to speak truth to us. Most of all, we keep our hearts by keeping our first love for Christ.

The rhythms and routines we follow to keep our hearts not only prepare us to preach, they do something even more important: they draw us closer to Christ. The perspectives and practices we embrace to keep our hearts are used by God to conform us into Christ's image, to change us "from one degree of glory to another" (2 Corinthians 3:18). As our lives increasingly reflect the glorious message we proclaim, the words on the plaque Bill Lawrence gave me ring true. We become the message. Our lives give voice to the truth we proclaim.

Preaching is hard work. That's no great revelation to anyone with an ongoing preaching ministry. What often comes as a surprise, and what I've tried to communicate in this book, is that the hardest work of preaching is the heart work it requires. But while heart work is demanding, it's also glorious. And it's enabled by grace. It's done in response to God's greater work for us, in us, and through us. As preachers, we keep our hearts because we know God keeps us. "Now to him who is able to keep you from stumbling and to present you blameless before the presence of his glory with great joy, to the only God, our Savior, through Jesus Christ our Lord, be glory, majesty, dominion, and authority, before all time and now and forever. Amen" (Jude 24–25).

AUTHOR/ SUBJECT INDEX

SCRIPTURE INDEX

OLD TESTAMENT